"L. A. is a Pilgrim, searching s of life. She invites you to join in her quest, and over the hilltop to meet Someone who said, "Seek, and you will find."
THE REVEREND DR. WILLIAM H. PHILIPS,
B.A., B.D, MTh., PhD., Presbyterian Pastor, retired

"This book will captivate those on a faith journey of discovery. L.A. is an expert storyteller...her words are relatable, honest, and inviting. She opens the flood gates of humble curiosity and fierce love to reveal that God is found in everyday living just as much (if not more) as within the structures of religion. If you have ever felt separated from God...if you have ever felt reluctant about the Divine's care for you...if you have ever felt alone, this book is the gift of belonging, courage, and love you have been waiting for. Your laughter and sorrows are all welcomed by God."
KRISTA POWERS,
MSW, Life Coach, Consultant, Author, Speaker

"...it invites tears and laughs and reflection all at once. Lovely and loving, and inviting love."
BRIAN SCHIRCLIFF,
M.S., Author, Co-Founder and Program
Director Vitality Buzz, Bliss, + Books

"What a ride! Readers will celebrate with L. A. as she is propelled by an "inner gentle force" to look for God in the daily events of her life. Her stories testify that she is a modern-day Hero of the Faith, perhaps a relic in her own right."
LOIS G.,
B.A., M.A., Director of Lifelong
Learning Institute, senior community resident

God is
in the Odd,
the Ordinary,
and Outside Church

By L. A. McMurray

Printed in the United States of America

First Printing, 2024

ISBN 978-1-955791-75-5

Library of Congress Control Number: 2024903477

Ordering Information: Special discounts are available on quantity purchases by bookstores, corporations, associations, and others. For details, contact the publisher at sales@ braughlerbooks.com or at 937-58-BOOKS.

For questions or comments about this book, please write to info@braughlerbooks.com.

Braughler Books
braughlerbooks.com

Dedicated to my Family

In loving memory of my father.

Acknowledgements

With much gratitude to the kind souls who graciously read multiple versions of this story over the years, and most especially those who held the story in their hearts with understanding and encouragement. Thank you, Anne, Annette, Bill, Bonita, Brian, Cayce, Colleen, David, Jack, Kim, Krista, Lois, Meredith, Nancy, and Sharon.

I wish to express my indebtedness to Sharon Roncone Velasquez, whose career in journalism and lifetime Catholic revised my manuscript with respect, honesty, and a wonderful sense of humor. Her sincere feedback and encouragement helped craft a uniquely inspiring story.

This story and my spirit grew exponentially because of L.L. Walker, with her gentle and wise leadership of our first bible study and forever friendship, we are eternally tethered souls.

Nancy LaFever, my editor, whose intellect, direction, and encouragement fine-tuned the details creating a tightly told tale.

Without Krista Powers, this book would still be in my file cabinet under "creative projects for the future." She pulled this out of my heart, organized thoughts, corralled my passion, and kept me on task to completion. She was a genuine cheerleader with every chapter and verse.

I am grateful for the positive enthusiasm from two college professors, one who told me I should be a writer and the other who said "...you made me laugh out loud."

A special thanks to Hailey Bollinger Photo who captured the exhilaration I feel in my yellow bug and the serenity of a golden sunset for my book cover.

Lastly, my deep appreciation for the patience, guidance, and professionalism of Braughler Books. Their commitment to my manuscript through the publishing process went above and beyond my greatest expectations.

1

*"Those we love don't go away, they walk beside us every day.
Unseen, unheard, but always near,
still loved, still missed, and very dear"*

Grandma Murphy
Irish Elder

An Irish Catholic walked into a shrine, in need of a direct sign from the divine within the golden walls, relics, and wine. Much to her dismay, it was not to be in that sacred space and time. Ah, but a few years later in her dusty and dog fur laden living room, the gentle whisper of the Almighty answered her anxious pleading soul with, "let it roll off your back."

Feeling blessed with her personal providential pep talk, she immediately applied heavenly wisdom resulting in one of the best holiday visits to date. Once her heart connected to the voice within, floodgates opened with profound serendipitous moments in the absurd, the ordinary, beyond church walls, the great outdoors, in cars and motorcycles.

The following pages delineate her circuitous scavenger hunt for God and genuine faith. This "she" I speak of is me, and thus my tale from Cradle Catholic to Spiritual Mystic. The pilgrimage began when I questioned religious hearsay and freed myself from generations of blind faith and layers of guilt. It required countless hours of conversation, questions, personal trials, and test-driving various denominations while Lucifer lurked in my rearview mirror.

It's not typical for a Catholic to discuss their personal religious experiences -- evangelism is an assignment bestowed on other denominations. Yet after spending time with people who spoke openly about their faith, I too freely shared my trust in God on numerous occasions with anyone, anywhere. Until the day I was silenced by a devout Catholic, who boldly stated, "People don't want to hear about that God stuff all the time."

Still recovering from a lifetime of Catholic structure, solid as cement, I share this spiritual journey from my discomfort zone with an internal tug of war between my heart and head. One force is pushing the narrative out, while the other keeps a vice grip on my soul's diary.

Half of me eagerly wants to be bold and declare to all that God is not confined to a building made of bricks or stone, and God cannot be defined or limited by human minds, nor exclusive to one chosen denomination, gender, nationality, or skin tone.

The other half squelches any zealousness because of a religion that chooses silence. At this writing, the power of the spiritual universe is winning and writing through my heart to anyone interested in my mystical, and mysterious adventure.

Let us begin with an example of one of the most profound spiritual encounters which happened the night after my father's funeral in 2018. It began while unpacking my luggage after returning from the extended weekend spent at my parents' home. My mental capacity was worn to a frazzle after weeks of caring for and about my terminally ill father, and my mother as his caregiver. His day by day, night after night, weakening of his body and spirit had been a front row seat to his death. If only we could have put a tourniquet on his suffering while hoping for a miracle.

As I stood by the ironing board, I flippantly muttered how I needed a break, not to eliminate thoughts of my dad, but a momentary pause from the horrendous pain of losing him. From the depth of my heartache sprang a cavalcade of divine timing and one of the holiest multi-layered mystical moments of my life.

A mental break for me is watching old movies, old being from the 1930s up to and through the '70s. I relish the intelligent screenplays, quality acting, decade-specific lingo and slang, silk dresses hugging the bone structure of emaciated actresses, iconic hairdos, art deco furniture, and classic cars. And who isn't uplifted by Doris Day or charmed by Cary Grant? It's self-care.

That evening, self-care was needed, unlike ever before, and I turned to my happy place, Turner Classic Movies, TCM, the classic movie channel on cable TV. It was several minutes past the start of the 8 p.m. feature movie with the brief introduction and behind-the-scenes trivia. Typically, I refuse to watch anything if I miss the beginning, but at this juncture the movie was irrelevant, what mattered most was the break from reality.

The movie was in color and appeared to be filmed in the 1960s era. I was intrigued by the crowd of women wearing designer suits and matching hats at a formal afternoon affair who were engaged in mind-numbing chatter about roses. Being born in the mid-sixties, clothes from that era speak to me, especially flower prints, vibrant colors, textures, and the ultimate in footwear - white go-go boots. I would wear them day and night if I could.

The next scene in the movie was a San Francisco street lined with cars from the late 1960s. The scene captured my attention for two reasons. One, my teenage daughter and I had just returned from our first ever girls' trip to California. She coordinated every detail from the location, accommodations, restaurants, and airport. My input was the credit card for payment.

Our plans were to fly into San Jose, rent a car, and enjoy five days in Pacific Grove, California. But two days before our trip, I visited with my parents and together we found on the Rand McNally Road Atlas exactly where our destination was in relation to some relatives who lived in California. It was at that moment I discovered how close we would be to San Francisco. I shared the proximity with my daughter and at the last minute we added one of the most famous west coast cities to our trip itinerary, just for one day.

Thinking about the trip brought a smile to my face considering how cool we thought we were pretending to be California girls driving a yellow Camaro convertible to and through the Golden Gate city.

Secondly, seeing the cars in the movie reminded me of my dad, he knew the make and model of every classic car. He used to buy cars, such as an MG, Corvair, or Austin Healy, and restore them for re-sale. He embraced the challenge of taking something broken and making it valuable again. He had an engineering mind, with the gift and talent of a car mechanic who respected the soul of the ride. He was in the sheet metal industry by trade, but his free time was spent in our garage "tinkering around" in his happy place.

The storyline of the movie went back inside the large historic home where the socialites mingled. The camera angle was through the panty-hosed legs of women carrying on multiple conversations, from pointed to pretentious, with snobby laughter. Then the camera zoomed in on a man leaning against the threshold of a doorway wearing a navy blue turtleneck, tan trench coat, dark pants, and a serious look on his face as he perused the crowd with intense blue eyes.

I recognized the actor as Steve McQueen and thought, I've never watched a Steve McQueen movie. He was not one of my favorites based solely on his macho themed movies and bad-boy reputation. I finished unpacking, settled on my bed, and then an odd inkling led me to search the web about him. This was strange because I rarely research biographies of actors and actresses, especially someone of no interest to me.

Yet, this one time I followed an internal curiosity. My heart pinched as I read the first headline that popped up, "Steve McQueen dies of complications from lung surgery to treat mesothelioma." Tears welled, as this was the same disease and post-surgery complications as my dad's diagnosis and, who, to the best we know, also died of mesothelioma.

Reading more, Steve McQueen's hobby and passion were classic cars and motorcycles. Same with my father. Learning more, Steve was a hot-headed Irishman, so was my father. Another article said he found Christ toward the end of his very tumultuous life. He attended church and died with a bible in his hand given to him by Billy Graham. I sensed something extraordinary fueling my curiosity.

I hit the guide button to see the title of this movie: it was Bullitt, labeled a mob murder mystery from 1968. I found multiple links about the movie, which held my full attention. The movie had the most iconic car chase in film history, lasting 11 minutes with no music, just the sound of car engines roaring and screeching tires. The car chase went through the very streets my daughter and I had just walked and drove through a few weeks prior, except in the movie they went a hair-raising, death-defying 100 mph. I did not.

The movie sported a green VW Beetle to ensure the car chase scenes were edited in the correct order. Ironically, I have a yellow VW Beetle and my father had a green miniature toy VW Beetle. One of the Mustangs used in this film had just been found in 2017 in a Tennessee barn owned by a private family, and Ford recently made a new edition of this exact Mustang, calling it "Bullitt" in honor of the movie's 50th anniversary.

My attempt to forget about losing my father vanished. This movie and the leading man reminded me of him more than ever, especially when I focused on the main character, San Francisco police detective Lieutenant Frank Bullitt, played by McQueen, who was solving a murder which involved the mob and a politician. It was hard to follow since I did not see it from the very beginning, but I liked Lt. Frank. He was caring, smart, protective, persistent, and a little unorthodox but always for the greater good. McQueen's character was very much like my own father.

The experience peeled back multiple layers and moments of serendipitous connections among the afterlife, with a classic Hollywood star, and his movie character, and recent events. My mind was tripping without the psychedelics!

During the car chase between Lt. Bullitt's green Mustang and the hitman's Dodge Charger, Frank Bullitt peeled the tires. My dad always asked me, and anyone who got a new car, "Did you peel the tires on it yet?!" I found his question annoying and predictable my whole life, but now it made me miss his voice and want to hear him ask me that question again, and again… a thousand times.

At the end of the movie, the murder was solved with the victim's fingerprints, and this was too much for my mind to comprehend, my father's presence solidified! My mom had ordered necklaces with my dad's thumbprint from the funeral home.

My soul filled like helium into a balloon. My mind grasped to fathom the compounding layers of how much this movie, this lead character, this actor, at this exact moment in my life completely and lovingly and very loudly stated, "Your dad is with you, he will always be with you!" I felt God and my father's presence, along with a myriad of angels collectively delivering a message from heaven via Steve McQueen. With the power of the spiritual cosmos, I was surrounded and comforted with eternal love, peace, and a holy presence. My bedroom was very crowded for this epiphany moment.

This experience brought to life the biblical quotation from Matthew 5:4 ESV, "Blessed are those who mourn, for they will be comforted." From beyond the grave, I was comforted as if cocooned by a king-size down comforter. Death can never take away the memories of my dad. In my brokenness, God responded and knew exactly what I needed when I needed it and how to deliver it – through a car chasing, mob murder mystery movie from 1968 starring Steve McQueen.

2

"Guilt is the gift that keeps on giving."

Erma Bombeck
Author

What did I do to deserve a personal telegram from heaven? Was it the luck of the Irish? Somewhat, according to Psalm 139:13 ESV "… you knitted me together in my mother's womb." With deep Irish lineage from both parents and grandparents, and being born on the same day as the feast of St. Brigid (a key saint in the Irish Culture), my mystical potential is off the charts.

More than my ancestry, the gift of God's presence that evening was because I was broken, completely shattered, and the Holy Word of God promises, "The Lord is close to the brokenhearted…" Psalm 34:18 ESV. The message was personal and specific just for me.

Celtic Spiritual history and knowledge of scripture were not known to me until years into my adulthood. Even though I was a cradle Catholic, a term used for those born and raised in a Catholic church, I didn't know God until I looked outside the church and within myself. Thus, it is my personal mission that my children and their children and their children's children, etc.…believe in the love and expansiveness of the Divine.

A key motivation behind writing this book is because I never knew my father was also a seeker of faith until years after his death. I wish he would have shared that with me when he was alive, and shame on me for not asking him while on my journey. The weight of guilt hangs heavy on my heart for not knowing more about my father as a person. My mom shared after his death that it was my Confirmation that inspired him to convert to Catholicism, and he always attended church even though his own parents didn't always do so. Fortunately, his heart for Jesus was obvious in the way he lived devoted and connected to family and friends. The real gift he left with me is to be Christlike in living and in action toward others without public declaration.

My father was a wonderful man, and I am forever grateful and honored to be his daughter. This book comes from a place of regret for not taking an interest in his life stories, especially his faith journey. I hope my children comprehend the significance of my spiritual walk, as I have learned to respect the history and deep spiritual roots of our ancestors.

My soul attempted to speak up decades ago through a restlessness and lack of connection to the Catholic mass. My regular attendance was out of guilt, fear and obligation. Then and now, many are disenchanted and disgusted by the church's abuse and scandalous history, garnering little value in religion. I understand where they sit.

Fortunate for all believers, to know that God is love, light, grace, and mercy does not require organized religion, nor a church building. Faith in and gratitude for a God who sees us with merciful eyes and an unconditional loving heart pulls back the veil between humanity on earth and the spiritual universe.

Spirit is everywhere in the odd, the ordinary, and a whisper away. This is my recollection of how I went from fearing eternity in Hades to living in the power of the Holy Spirit every minute of each day and knowing full well that there is more to faith than Sunday mass. Historically in the Catholic religion, that one hour at church is the be all and end all of worship and the only place to find God. But, the reality is, the other 167 hours of the week matter even more.

I will start my story with a confession: forgive me, but I've hated church most of my life. It began as a child with suffocating car rides filled with cigarette smoke in our Chevy Impala on the longest five-minute drive to St. Charles. Followed by a child's standard of inhumane treatment of cartilage crunching kneeling on bare wood, butt-numbing wooden pews, extreme quiet for 60 minutes, and the hypnotic trance caused by the monotonous blah blah blah of the priest. Making matters worse was that my mother preferred the front row. As if being closest to the altar made us closer to God.

When I was young, and on many occasions to this day, my vision blurs once the priest starts his homily. The lights dull and my eyes play tricks on me as people come in and out of focus. It's as if a fog settles on the altar, filling the atmosphere with a haze.

Over the years, some priests appear angry, others haughty, or bored, or secretly miserable. Maybe their stiff collars pressed against their Adam's apple make it difficult to breathe, speak, and be holy all at once. My thoughts, and not very empathetic ones, are – if they were going to torture me for an hour, it only seems fair they suffer too.

Their words often jumbled together in a stream of nonsense. Most times whatever they were talking about did not pertain to me; I was too young. Church was geared to adults who had the capacity for self-control, redundant ceremonies, and religious obligations.

As a child I was suspect of the statues of Jesus, Mary, Joseph, the monks, and saints scattered throughout the church. I questioned if their eyes were spying on me, judging my ability to pay attention, and keeping attendance records.

My spiritual wrestling match continued through middle school when I started to wrangle with religious dogma. My first face-to-face confession prior to making my confirmation went something like this, me: "Why can't women be priests? And why are nuns sworn to poverty when priests aren't? And why are nuns limited to teaching, but priests are head of churches, regions, and potentially a Pope?" Priest: sniffs and snorts with intense aggravation, lips pursed, piercing eyes, "Do you have any sins to confess?" The man of the cloth cut me to the quick.

The act of confession always proved challenging, especially as a child and well-behaved adolescent, what could I have done wrong? I did not break any of the Ten Commandments. What else was there? Every time I sat in the claustrophobic wooden closet, I found myself examining the doll house-sized velvet curtain within inches of my face. I pondered and questioned, not my heart for sin, but if that curtain and screen were enough to protect my identity and disguise my voice. As if such anonymity was needed at that age.

Often, I made something up: like I disobeyed my parents, or I took something that belonged to my sister. But when I had not done either of those sinful acts, I was lying to the priest about lying and stealing. And that felt like a real sin, so my confession was appropriate for lying about lying when I really had not lied at all. I considered the entire process as sin neutral.

3

"Change your thoughts and you change your world."

Norman Vincent Peale
Author

The most interesting church experiences happened when I attended different denominations. Like the time our babysitter took my sister and me to a Baptist Revival Meeting. We were young and very impressionable, and I never forgot the details. The music was loud and upbeat, and people frequently and randomly shouted "AMEN!" from their seats, raising their outstretched arms and waving their hands back and forth in the air expressing overwhelming approval toward the preacher who hadn't even started his sermon.

The collective choir with multitudes of people were able to hold a tune while simultaneously swaying in unison wearing long robes. With their feet stomping and voices bellowing, the church vibrated shaking the foundation beneath my feet.

The entire congregation was smiling, singing joyfully as if it were the best day of their lives. They clapped to the music, some danced in place, and some unable to contain themselves overflowed into the aisles. There was enough activity and praising all around to keep my attention for more than an hour, the exact opposite of our church service, and I loved the energy and collective feeling of happiness. But I knew better: real church was not a happy place.

Another time when I was in middle school, my sister and I went with our cousin to her Pentecostal church which was more like a holy circus. Some guy in front of us raised his arms, looked up to the ceiling and yelled nonsensical words. It was wild, off the wall, and totally goofy which made me laugh hysterically. My sister thought I was being rude and gave me a stiff elbow into my ribcage, but when a giggle comes from the gut at an inappropriate time, there's no way to contain it. In my mind, if a person shouts in church, where people are not even supposed to talk, then he was asking for weird looks and laughter.

At one point, people moved like a herd of cattle up the aisle toward the front of the church. Similar to a Black Friday free-for-all Communion sale, but this church wasn't distributing Communion. People around us were crying with their heads bowed down. I had no clue why or what caused such a reaction. Others raised one hand in the air with the other clutched to their chest, as if asking a question while having chest pains.

One guy fell to his knees at the altar, and like carp racing to bread in a pond, a group of people surrounded him putting their hands all over him. Did he break something in the fall or was he the most horrific sinner they pushed to the floor? It was frustrating because I was too short to see everything that was occurring, I started jumping up and down, getting higher with each jump to get a better look at the chaos. My sister kept pulling me back down by my shirt. Ignoring her, I leapt from my tippy toes to watch the carnival.

I looked at my cousin, and asked "WOW, is this how your church is all the time?!" She just smiled, not confirming, or denying it. Certainly, in my mind, the Pentecostals and Baptists did not "do church" correctly, but they did provide outstanding entertainment.

I always thought God was more likely to be out there, high in the clouds somewhere. I pictured him with an attendance book, like my schoolteachers with the dates across the top and names listed down the left side. We receieved green check marks for attending mass and a solid red "X" for being absent, more red marks confirmed eternity in the lake of fire upon one's last breath.

Attending mass as a child, my attention varied from the stained-glass windows to people's shoes as they passed by during Communion, or the way people dressed and women's hairdos. My focus as a teenager was solely looking around at cute boys, be they altar boys or scattered throughout the congregation. One teen boy in particular, (Sweet Jesus, he was incredible!), Buddy Applegate.

Buddy was a few years older than me and without doubt and debate the cutest boy in church; teenage heartthrob gorgeous. His unkempt curly brown hair, long enough to touch his shirt collar, resembled Jim Morrison of The Doors. His broad, muscular shoulders stretched the cotton fibers of his shirt, giving an outline of his sculpted physique. Top that off with his breath-taking smile, perfect teeth, plump lips, and the best backside that ever filled a pair of Jordache Jeans, and you've got yourself a fine teenage specimen of God's creation. I fully enjoyed the view from head to hamstrings.

When he sat in front of me, my heart beat faster and faster out of my chest with every moment closer to when the priest directed the congregation to "share with one another the Sign of Peace." Anticipating that gesture of shaking hands with him was the height of excitement for this teenager. Our hands would embrace, our eyes would meet, and my heart would flutter. Sometimes he crushed my young spirit when he didn't turn around to give me the Sign of Peace. However, on the good fortune when I stood in front of him, I had control and never missed an opportunity to place my handful of peace into his hand, only after I gave peace to my sister first to wipe off the sweat. Buddy made mass worth attending.

During high school and college, I took myself to church, not because I wanted to attend, but out of obligation to my parents, and the constant fear of going to hell. I usually arrived late, sat in the back, left after Communion, and totally avoided Confession all together. I considered my attendance record clean and in good standing. Catholics are taught it is a mortal sin to miss Catholic mass on Sunday and that God is in the Tabernacle, a golden locked box, and priests deliver The Divine to the congregation through Communion. That is what I knew of God for most of my life: in a box, out of reach, priests were the gatekeepers, and being in church hopefully made me good enough to get into Heaven.

Once while babysitting, I found a book on their bookshelf The Power of Positive Thinking by Dr. Norman Vincent Peale. This introduced me to using positive quotes from the bible for life's difficulties.

The quick affirmations were easily pulled into my teenage drama and offered momentary peace. But it wasn't something I maintained.

Speaking of theatrics, being forced to look at the oversized crucified Jesus on a cross dangling from the ceiling had lasting shock value. It was disturbing to see him half-naked and in such agony week after week for an hour. Each time I looked at the bloody nailed hands, feet, and lifeless head of Jesus, I quickly turned away as if passing an awful car accident.

And so it went, attending mass year after year, with the same useless monotone homilies, distracted thoughts, fashions changing, priests coming and going, and of course, the music remained horribly the same.

I lived with the weight of suspicion that God looked down on me, waiting for me to do something wrong and when I did, he made a note in "the Book" and zapped me with something to teach me a lesson.

One time, I missed mass two weeks in a row and then came down with eczema all over my face. It was nasty… the itching, the puss-filled acne, the redness, and it was my own fault. I had no excuse for missing church. Well, I had an excellent excuse; I was hungover on Sunday from going out with friends the night before.

4

"Go to heaven for the climate, hell for the company."

Mark Twain
Author

Once when I was in sixth grade, I naively attended a youth group with a Presbyterian friend. Unaware of differences between denominations, I seized the opportunity to meet new boys my age. That night began with a friendly welcome, which was nice, but I was more impressed with the snack table full of cookies. Sign me up for this church.

The first activity was to go around the circle and say our name, age, school, and church we attended. All was going well, until I shared my personal information which prompted a collective gasp and cocking of heads toward me, followed by a solid hush in the basement meeting space.

One girl lifted her eyebrows to clarify what she heard, "St. Charles?!" Initiating a barrage of questions and accusations from her and the rest of the group calling me a statue worshiper, and not "saved," and going to hell if I am not baptized and dunked in the baptismal pool to be born again.

I knew I was baptized as a baby, but what does "born again" mean? Others started making absurd statements like, "You like Mary more than Jesus." And "You worship saints, and that's idolatry." I may have been young, but I suddenly felt akin to the women falsely tried at the Salem Witch trials.

The cute boy sitting next to me slid safely in the other direction and explained, "You have gravened images in your church and that breaks a Ten Commandment!"

When the introductions were over, I couldn't exit up the stairs fast enough, but not without swiping the remaining cookies. Their words and judgement lingered on my mind for years.

I thought I had moved on, until college and that memory rose to the occasion and potentially proved those kids right.

I was a member of the chorus line for our college musical production. One day during rehearsals, the two leads were on stage while the rest of the cast took a break. I remained in the theatre to soak up the whole performance experience. Another cast member, my dance partner, followed me to the seats as we watched the two leads practice their lines.

I mentioned how much I respected their God-given talent. He started bouncing up and down in the spring seat exuberantly sharing he was a believer too and how he was saved after accepting Christ as his savior. He explained he overcame his shady past of drinking and barhopping. I didn't think those were something in need of being saved from. The more he continued with his "testimony" the more I wanted saved from this conversation. My mind traveled back to the youth groups' verbal attack, and kept my mouth shut about my religiosity.

After rehearsal, the lead actress told the female cast she was giving us a psychological quiz. Since psyche was my minor, I was all in.

She asked us a series of four questions. We were to list our favorite animal, color, body of water, and the last one was to describe our feelings as if we were alone in an all-white room. We made our lists, then she explained the meaning of our answers. The animal is how others see us, the color is how we see ourselves, the body of water is what we like about sex. That was worth a chuckle and embarrassing revelations. And then she explained the last one being how we will feel upon our death.

Feminine collegiate laughter echoed through the locker room, except from me, because on my slip of paper was, "punished, lonely, isolated, tortured."

I gasped, my adjectives were likened to those used to describe eternity in hell. I am going to the lake of fire when I die. My subconscious knew my destiny, that youth group predicted it, and the pop quiz proved my greatest fear: eternal damnation.

While in college, I began to question what I considered manmade rules in our church and how there were different ones for Catholics, Protestants, Latter Day Saints, Baptists, Nazarene, Pentecostals, etc. Every religion had different criteria that prequalified one for heaven, but which one should we aspire to follow? Certainly, adhering to the incorrect checklist had dire consequences, and ignorance secured a hot tub in Hades. Fear fogged my brain much like a dense cloud hovers over an open field.

Who was right? A girl in my elementary school was not allowed to celebrate her birthday or any holiday because of her "religion." Others were forbidden to go to the movie theater or dance because of church beliefs. What about the Jewish people who do not believe in Jesus, or the peaceful life of Buddhism, or the Mormons who have their own book authored by some guy they followed westward ho. Who had the correct formula and, more importantly, which one of us would partake in the perpetual bonfire or rest peacefully on a fluffy cloud?

There had to be someone who could clarify which were the actual rules. Perhaps a psychic or one of the religion professors. After considering all the experts I knew, it hit me. The best person was Father John, a monk who performed Catholic mass outside along the border of Mill Creek Park and outside of the Diocese of Youngstown's approval. The bishop did not recognize Father John's mass as "counting for church" because he disapproved of Father John's unorthodox ways, the monastery, and how much everyone loved the monk.

I never knew the real story behind his ostracization, and never cared because mass at the monastery was brief, to the point with relatable homilies, and only 30 to 45 minutes, max. It was perfect, in and out and my duty was done for the week.

Fortunately for me, Father John frequented the fitness center where I worked, so after one of his scheduled racquetball matches, I took advantage of the opportunity to seek his wisdom. I approached him with equal measure of caution and careless confidence.

He was a large man at least 6'5" and around 220 pounds, which only made his presence more commanding and exactly what I pictured God to look like: an exceptionally large, grey- haired, wise, old man. The difference between God and Father John was that Father John smiled and was friendly, and I knew God was angry and disapproved of everything I found fun.

I started right away, "I want the golden ticket into heaven with fire insurance. I am so confused about the different rules for different religions. How do we know which ones are right?" I continued with the list of confusing rules. Father John nodded, smiled with a contemplative look like he understood my concern, yet never interrupted my lengthy rant.

I explained about the recent quiz and how there was a high probability I was going to hell, and I do not even know why because I was a good girl. I never had one detention in school and perfect attendance most years. I've never hurt anyone, with one exception, when babysitting, I turned to throw away the dirty diaper and the baby rolled off the changing table and SPLAT - she rolled off and, she smacked hard onto the wooden floor. Thankfully, she was okay, and it certainly wasn't premeditated or intentional.

I have only stolen once when I took extra pieces of paper at the library, the little forms for the librarian to help someone find a book. I took a whole pile home with me; my mom made me take them back and apologize. I hoped those two incidents were not on my permanent spiritual record.

I mentioned someone else I knew who went to church activities on Saturday, attended two services on Sunday, again on Wednesday night, and sometimes other events at the church throughout the week. Perhaps I wasn't attending church enough.

Then Father John gently turned his head toward me and put his hand on mine and said "There are only two things you need to focus on: love God and love each other. That's it. God says to love Him with all your heart, mind, soul, and strength. And to love our neighbor. It's that simple. You do those two things, and you will be fine."

Really?! Piece of cake. I was liberated from following a tyrannical set of rules, and handed a free pass to drink, dance, cuss, enjoy movies, celebrate birthdays, and read comic strips.

5

"I'm in HOT PURSUIT!"

Sheriff Bufford T. Justice
"Smokey and the Bandit"

I met my husband in high school. Both being from Catholic homes, part of our dating routine included going to mass on Sunday mornings, NOT at 7:30 a.m. when my parents went, but to the latest morning service at our home church beginning at 11:15 a.m., or to 11:30 a.m. at the monastery near the park with Father John. And on some occasions when the sun arose too soon after a late night, we squeaked in the very last opportunity on Sunday evening at 5:15 p.m. held at St. Patrick's in the older part of Youngstown where our grandparents grew up.

If we went in the morning, our plans included going out for breakfast. I always hoped our dates lasted all day and into the evening, because I could not get enough of my sweetheart. He was funny, *the* most handsome man ever (even more than Buddy), was ambitious, gregarious, and had a great family. To me, he was perfect.

Our families, both parents and grandparents were labeled "practicing Catholics" because they attended mass religiously, sometimes daily and at the very least, weekly, plus they gave monetarily to the church – the true measurement of commitment by the diocese.

We dated through college and married in the same church where we both made our First Holy Communion and Confirmations. Our family quickly grew from the two of us with one dog, to four children and multiple dogs. Over the years, we did our due diligence getting our family of six up and out the door on Sunday mornings and sometimes interrupting a perfectly good Saturday afternoon.

The pressure for me to avoid hell lay dormant in my mind and then reared its ugly head as I assumed the responsibility to keep my children from the same fate. I used every bit of my blessed mother power to protect my children from the fires of hell and if that meant waking them from a deep weekend slumber or pulling them away from a sunny afternoon in the backyard, then so be it.

Admittedly, church experiences felt like hell on earth. The flames began with trying to get everyone ready and out the door on time, which rarely happened. There is no measure for how hard it is to arrive inconspicuously at church with four young children, an angry mother carrying loads of equipment, and a perfectly calm husband trailing behind at a snail's pace.

If everyone understood the heavy lift in coordinating a family to get out of the house, fully dressed, semi-clean, every Sunday morning then there would be fewer snarls and judgmental jeers from the pews.

Sitting still was not in my, nor my children's genetic code. Of course, I expected my children to do something I was incapable of doing, and instinctively darted parental stares of "Don't you dare touch your brother/sister!" and "Stop squirming!" and the always pleading/piercing look of "PAY ATTENTION!"

Countless services were spent with me or my husband removing one of our children to the back of the church with the rest of the crying, screaming, inconsolable children and their exasperated parents. We could not hear what was going on or being said, but by God we were there. And at this phase in our lives, that was enough.

Our oldest children were basically well behaved in church. The younger two...not so much, our daughter's screams echoed and reverberated off every wall. However, it was the pre-church that aggravated me the most. My husband's lack of punctuality drove me nuts, and my anger brewed along with his multiple cups of coffee while I washed and dressed every child. It was a good thing we went to church, because I broke every Beatitude before breakfast.

One unforgettable Sunday morning, as usual we arrived late. None of us wanted to be there, and our daughter was being extremely vocal about her feelings with ear-piercing shrills and crying. Lord have mercy, she knew how to express herself. I was with her in the Narthex of the church, after removing ourselves from the rest of the congregation due to her decibel level.

While I did my best to keep our then two-year-old daughter entertained and quiet in the safe zone, there was a nun standing near us giving me the stink eye. She stood staunch and proud of her role as holy hall monitor, taking mental notes on the parents failing to control their children. She was in her designated area of patrol and more than eager to raise an eyebrow to anyone who arrived late and/or left early, i.e., right after communion.

I was holding my precious girl in my arms, but my arms got tired, and I had to put her down. And that is when my sweet child took complete advantage of my exhaustion and sprinted down the center aisle straight toward the altar with the pontificating priest. She was fast and I thought she would turn around and return when she became too far from me. She did not, and when she was halfway down the aisle, the nun took off to bring her back, forcing me to take off after the Nun of the Narthex.

Both of us were in hot pursuit of a toddler. The world turned into slow motion and my arms reached for my daughter, but they weren't long enough to grab around the nun and retrieve the back of my daughter's neck or clothing, or hair, anything to end this public display of an undisciplined child.

The nun was a stride ahead of me, in power and determination to capture this impetuous child as if the situation was her responsibility. I was embarrassed, and that was *my* child she was chasing. We were equally motivated yet fueled by a different fire. The nun kept the advantage ahead of me, until I saw the look in her eyes when she turned to see where I was, then my momma bear instincts took over. I leapt next to her and may have used an elbow to get her out of the way for me to gain the advantage and nab my daughter just shy of the altar.

Returning to the back of the church with my daughter firmly in my arms, I made eye contact solely with the wooden floor. The winded nun nipped the back of our heels like a wayward grocery cart. Huffing and puffing her way to the sacred lobby where she explained sternly,

"Father does NOT like noisy, disruptive children in mass."

I didn't respond. My daughter was two years old and had no comprehension of the priest's unrealistic expectations of children's behavior in this stifling environment. She was not deliberately disruptive, although she was a very smart child and probably knew exactly what she was doing, but really, she was just acting like every other two-year-old being held against their will.

6

"Our first teacher is our own heart."

Wisdom of the Cheyenne tribe

My full time job outside the home was in pharmaceutical sales, where we make sales calls to hospitals, clinics, physicians' offices, and pharmacies. Our territories vary in size according to the diseases and drugs we market. My territory had the largest geography in our district, measuring multiple counties, taking three hours to drive from one end to the other. In most accounts, we are as welcome as the transient door-to-door salesman arriving during the weekday dinner hour. Understandably, some reps have tainted the general opinion of us due to their stalking tactics in parking lots, excessive appearances, and disrespecting staff to get to the doctor.

Listening to the radio helped pass the time and overcome the beatdown of glass windows being slammed shut on my face by power hungry gate keepers. My musical taste spanned the spectrum, anything from Broadway show tunes to pop to classical; it just depended on my mood in that moment.

My first company car, a basic reliable Ford Taurus from the mid-90s, never had a CD player to enjoy my preferred music, forcing me to listen to whatever came in clearly over the airwaves. I am a "seeker" when it comes to many things, especially with the radio, my mood changes quickly and the song must adjust. Plus, at the first sound of static, my index finger hits the seek button until it stops on a clear station. If the tune doesn't fit my feeling, push the button, push, push again until the right tune matched my state of mind. In my rural geography, it was extremely difficult to keep a station static-free for more than thirty minutes at a time, let alone find something worth listening to.

One day while traveling to Bellefontaine, a town about an hour northwest of Columbus, Ohio with a population of approximately 13,000, the radio surfing began; push button, commercial, push button, another commercial, push button, country music, quickly push button, then a very loud and animated mature male voice shouted something and my finger stopped pushing the button.

He was so exaggerated, it sounded like a comedy routine. I immediately accepted this gift of humor from the radio gods and listened for a good laugh. He was talking about David and Goliath, the biblical story. His voice and delivery took my mind to the church scene in The Blues Brothers movie with James Brown as the preacher.

Something held my finger away from the seek button, maintaining the healing moment of healthy laughter. But, then without realizing it, I stopped laughing and was drawn into the story.

He boldly stated, "The story of David and Goliath is one that all of us can relate. We all have giants in our lives, anything we come up against can be considered a giant. Think about the giants in your life, perhaps a challenge you are facing, or an obstacle, or a constant struggle. Maybe it's financial debt, broken relationships, drug addiction, your job." I was dangling on his hook.

His pregnant pauses kept my attention, then he posed questions directed at the listening audience applicable to modern life. He inquired about our attitude and level of faith, and if our faith is comparable to David's, who found strength and confidence to take on the giant. He explained with great clarity and boldness that David's belief was grounded in the power of God.

The preacher took in long deep breaths, requiring extra air for his dynamic delivery. After the oxygen reload, he drilled home the facts about David's unshakable faith, the obstacles he overcame, having a trusting attitude, and living with the unimaginable power of God.

He made comparisons to addictions, lack of family and friends' support, and other common struggles experienced by every living being.

By now, I was hook, line, and sinker into his story. I lost the movie scene in my head and felt swept away by this interpretation of David defeating Goliath. While consuming this religious story disguised as a motivational message, a speck of intrigue pulled me further into his sermon.

I started talking back to the radio, "Keep talking, Mr. Preacher Man. I hear you, and I am getting this." He continued with more scripture and more inspiring words relating one's faith and ability to overcome tests and obstacles when we keep God at the center of our heart and energy.

I arrived at the location of my appointment early enough to keep listening. This office was near the boat docks of Indian Lake and the parking lot overlooked the small marina. The waterfront was a welcome setting to my momentous epiphany of understanding a religious story. Turning off the car engine was out of the question, I had to to keep listening to the rest of the program.

He concluded that an undeniable faith comes from knowing and trusting in God's Holy Word and promises.

Mesmerized by a voice on the radio, a biblical message, the sparkling water, and the excitement stirring within was all so strange. There was a tiny flicker inside of me, this same feeling I had when I was young and repeated bedtime prayers, or that internal direction to follow the right rules.

My awe at this radio moment by the lake turned into elation. His words were inspiring and enlightening, but then my attitude flipped to agitated because why couldn't priests give sermons in a way that grabbed my attention like this man. I was confused about why I was enjoying a religious experience when it was not even on a Sunday, and nowhere near a church. I was in my company car by a shallow lake, outside of a doctor's office. I paused to fathom the unexpected experience.

I wanted whatever was arising within to continue. The program, the surprise, the excitement, the learning, the relating...all of it. Even though the program ended, I didn't dare change the channel and yearned for another spirit stirring serendipitous program to follow.

I was greedy for more, then felt guilty for being greedy, wondering if there was such a thing as "good greed" when it was spiritual. My mind swirled between reality and spirituality, but I should have been thinking about punctuality because I missed my appointment.

My head and heart shifted from the beginning of the program to the end. Curiosity brewed, and I wanted more, to hear more, to know more and keep riding this soul rising wave.

As the next program was being introduced, my hopes were high. The program that had just ended and the one about to begin were men with doctorate degrees in theology. Since both radio preachers had Dr. in front of their names, I counted them as sales calls.

The next preacher was not as animated as the previous preacher, but I gave him a chance. To my delight, he did not disappoint. Throughout his sermon he spoke with a slight southern accent, nor was he boring, or condemning. He wasn't pretentious or confusing by circling around the subject matter with mindless streaming religious words above my head.

He explained how the bible was the living word of God and the resource for life. It was the place for answers, regardless of circumstances or crisis, and God will take a situation and turn it for good. All we need is to believe in Him, his son, Jesus Christ, and the Holy Spirit who lives within each of us. I believe in God, perhaps that is who took my finger off the radio dial, and why my ears pricked, and was magnetized to these two men. I looked around and wondered, "Is God in my car?"

He asked the listening audience if we were living in fear, anxiety, and full of worry. I shouted at that dashboard, "YES! I am. Right here, right now, always have been and probably always will be!" He then quoted 2 Timothy 1:7 NKJV, "For God has not given us a spirit of fear, but of power, and of love, and of a sound mind."

My head tilted like a dog who lifts his ears when he hears something strange. I questioned that statement because I knew plenty of church goers who struggle with worry and anxiety. My own grandmother was afraid and anxious about everything yet she never missed mass. Worrying was a way of life in my family, stretching back several generations, fear was a part of my fiber and family crest. Could this random radio preacher be preaching something that could help me with this? I found it odd because I never considered anxiety to be a religious problem; it was more a personality trait than a need for Jesus thing.

I was born free spirited, flowers in my hair, living without a care, traveling everywhere the music, wind, and sunshine took me. Then life, love, and a baby carriage happened, and with one flip of a gestational switch, I turned into the most neurotic, over-protective, worry warrior in the world.

Since the birth of my children, I have been consumed with fear. Will they be healthy or have special needs? What if they get sick? What if they get hurt? What if someone bullies them or God forbid, they get abducted? Worse case scenarios constantly filled my head. According to my logic I was being a good momma considering every situation. Thinking about it often enough gave me the preparation for when it did happen. This intense protective parenting demonstrated how much I cared about our children.

Radio preacher #2 spoke like a caring and kind grandfather with empathy, confidence, and a willingness to share meaningful life wisdom born from personal experience. He wasn't condemning me for worrying, he gently explained a better way of living.

He spoke of God offering a life free of fear and anxiety and the game plan was to believe, obey, and trust in the divine holy word. There's another plug for the bible. He made it sound like a good read. Why don't our priests encourage reading the bible? More importantly, does God really care about me being a worrywart?'

The program ended with him asking if we believed in Jesus. Of course, I did. He hung on the cross at church, we celebrate his birth at Christmas and honor his horrible death and glorious resurrection with delicious chocolate on Easter. Then he asked listeners to repeat a short and simple prayer to be considered born again and officially added to God's good list.

"Born again," there it was again. This time when I heard those words, something strange happened in my car that hour, unable to name it only feel it. Jesus healed the sick, but he was not on my official physicians list, nor on my call plans for the day. I was in a speck on a map size town being pulled into unfamiliar radio programs completely unclear what was happening. My nerves settled at the same time anticipation stirred.

Unsure of what he meant by being born again or the Book of Lambs or being saved, but when he told us to repeat after him, I did.

I just sat there by Indian Lake, supposedly making sales calls, but unable to move. No one forced me to listen. This was between me, two strangers on the radio, and an inner gentle force tapping on my soul.

7

"A questioning man is halfway to being wise."

Irish Proverb

My spirit yearned for more, more than the church was offering. Unsure if it was a need for inspiring sermons or just better music, or that I had tired of the routine and "obligation" – the term used by the church for weekend and designated holy days' attendance. While growing up, and to this very day, priests remind parishioners that it is a "sin" to miss weekend Catholic church services. And if a holy day falls on a weekend, we are expected to attend mass multiple times on the same day. Furthermore, if attending a wedding or funeral, even with a full mass, that doesn't count as one's attendance if it is held before the diocese determined time, usually prior to 4:00pm on a Saturday.

When I attend an event out of obligation there is a reluctance, almost a dread and disconnection. However, when attending events where I actually want to be, it brings forth excitement, positive anticipation, and an open heart. My attitude toward mass carried the same level of dread as attending a weekly staff meeting, it was necessary, sometimes useful, but always insufferable.

Being in pharmaceutical sales, I drove countless hours making sales calls throughout God's green Ohio acres. After discovering Christian radio and contemporary Christian music, it became my radio station of choice. I reasoned that it gave me extra credit in the religion attendance book since it was above and beyond the expected holy days of obligation.

My desire to listen to religious people and songs in my car during the week felt twisted because I had nary a miniscule of motivation to attend mass. My sole purpose for being present in church was to be good enough to get me and my family into heaven. Instinctively I knew it was in our best interest to attend versus not. Of course, I questioned what was pulling me into these work-week sermons.

One day while driving from Coldwater to Sydney, there were signs for the Maria Stein Shrine. The rhyme itself captivated me. Even more enticing was the teaser that it possessed one of the largest, documented collections of holy relics in the United States. In the Catholic religion, relics are a thing…a big thing… a sacred thing, but to me…a confusing thing. These special objects are classified on multiple levels, including first, second, and third class. The definition of a relic is "something left behind by a holy person" and there is a coding system for further clarification, and from my viewpoint…greater intrigue.

A first-class relic is part of the saint's body (not sure if that is legal, ethical, or sanitary), a second-class relic is something owned by the saint (think memorabilia), and a third-class relic is an object which has been touched to a first or second-class relic or by a saint (think pawn shop items, refer to an authority to confirm authenticity).

As soon as the Maria Stein Shrine came into view, there was a slight uptick in my adrenaline with the expectation of upping my spiritual game. People who have had visions of Mary were considered blessed, nominated for sainthood, and able to sell a lot of trinkets to go along with their stardom including candles, medals, statues, and coins. I wanted to be one of those blessed people who saw a divine vision, thus explaining why I veered off my course of a typical workday, to go on a voyage to find my "sign" at the Maria Stein Shrine.

The church and retreat center were not far from the main road, which was a two-lane highway in the middle of rural farmland. Stones crunched like potato chips under my tires as I pulled into the gravel lot and parked under the gift shop sign. Everything in me wanted to have an experience, a vision, something that affirmed God's presence and that he really cared about me the way the radio preachers promised.

There was a scattering of people kneeling and praying, but not many, most likely because it was the middle of the afternoon on a weekday. My heels clicked on the hard wood floor and echoed through the church as I walked the extensive center aisle to find a pew in which to pray.

Inside the large sanctuary were elongated stained glass windows, a strong scent of cedar from the historic wood structure, and a soaring high ceiling.

On the altar were three distinct levels of wooden chairs with backs of varying heights, they were a mix of thrones fit for royalty or Goldilocks' three bears. The tallest one with a big cushion, the medium one with a thinner cushion, and the smallest one was cushion less.

The ceiling contained dark wooden beams crisscrossing like a sky version of tic-tac-toe. Of most interest to me was a smaller private space to the right toward the front of the church. Being curious, I slowly tip-tapped my way over where there were only a few wooden pews. Once upon the select space, my eyes widened with wonder at the plethora of candles, small statues, gold chalices, various sizes of crosses, and one of the most bizarre sites I ever saw in or out of a church…a glass box display case the size and shape of casket with a petite woman's body lying face up inside. She was dressed in a Tibetan style red silk pantsuit with gold stitching and wearing jewelry. I found Maria Stein…or did I?

No, I did not. As I read the plaque, it explained this was the bodily remains of St. Victoria, a martyr of the early church (c. 304) covered in wax. I gasped! Was her real body covered in wax or was she a wax figure like those in Madame Tussauds Wax Museum? The jury is still out. Reading more, I learned that she is honored for her refusal of an arranged marriage. On her wedding day she leapt from a window in her parents' house, was arrested for her faith, and later executed. The rings on her finger were placed there as acts of piety, a symbol to others that she was religious, like my cross jewelry does for me.

Her hands were positioned specifically to represent a person of nobility and for martyrs who immediately join the ranks of Christ's noble company of saints. She was the original runaway bride. As unfortunate as her death was for standing up in defiance of an arranged marriage and for her faith, she won in the end when awarded sainthood, a goal of all practicing Catholics, and was laid to rest in a glass coffin in an Ohio town with one traffic light.

St. Victoria in her clear encasement was very odd, but it was a holy kind of odd and the perfect sort of strange when witnessing something divine from God. I decided kneeling would improve the chances of something special happening. My gaze zeroed in on this mysterious woman, mentally encouraging her to give me a sign. Nothing happened. I looked around at the other relics, wondering which one had the most power, which one would do something so that I could be "the one" who had a vision to report to people.

I closed my eyes and bowed my head in prayer, asking God, pleading with God, "Give me a sign like those in Medugorje, Lourdes or Fatima. Tell me something, show me something… anything." I concentrated all the mental power within my cranium. However, after a few seconds of straining, I realized one cannot witness a vision with one's eyes closed. I quickly opened my eyes and stared back at Victoria, hoping she would sit up and tap on the glass, start crying, or give me a royal wave bending from the wrist.

I watched her without blinking from the top of her adorned head to the tips of her black ballet slippers, telepathically coaxing a heel turn from one dancer to another. Nothing. I moved my focus from her feet to her hands, centering my focus on those jeweled fingers. I felt the anticipation of a baseball pitcher waiting on the catcher to signal which type of ball to throw.

I whispered, "Come on, lady, do something, two thumbs up, or the most apropos - the peace sign. You have multiple options, use one of them. I was a frightened bride once too, who isn't afraid of marriage? Unlike you though, I never ran away or jumped out a window. That should get me some acknowledgment." Nothing. Perhaps her glass case was sound proof.

My eyes wandered to her head hoping for facial movement, a blink, a smile, a twitch, a wiggle of her nose. Nary a nod. My attention turned away from her and to every miniature infant Jesus statue, golden chalice, cross, metal box, anything that might suddenly do something to prove God was up there listening and watching me watching them. Nay.

I stood up slowly, giving the Snow White look alike plenty of time and opportunity to make a bigger name for herself. She refused my mental telepathy. I murmured "YOU, Ms. Victoria, may be a first-class relic, but to me you are a first-class fake." I lingered a little longer, hoping, hoping for a blessed moment. When nothing occured in my alloted time, I gave up.

If relics are considered sacred and hold religious significance, then why wasn't anything powerful happening here?! Over 1,000 relics of gold, intricately carved wood, hand-painted porcelain, a wax body, historical one-of-a-kind artifacts and not one threw me a bone.

Walking back down the center aisle of the church toward the gift shop, I noticed a side door that led to a courtyard outside. It was one of those perfectly chilled spring days with intermittent puffy clouds and the sun radiating just enough warmth, I accepted nature's invitation to meet outside. There had to be something special about this place. Although I had not found my specific vision yet, my treasure hunt continued.

A short walk led me to an area between the main church and the retreat center. This section of the grounds included multiple giant stone statues arranged in a circle to face each other. My hopes grew higher than these ginormous stones who held the potential of cracking as my big sign. While standing in the middle of the circle I stopped to guess who each statue represented. I assumed they were various saints and the three wise men, but after I counted, I deducted they were probably the twelve disciples from the Last Supper.

Each stone man measured at least eight feet tall and stood on top of a three-foot concrete pedestal, my neck got a kink in it as I strained to look up at their oversized, hardened chiseled faces.

And look I did. I trained my gaze on each face long enough for them to give me an indication that he was my sanctified experience, blessing me with a special message. When one did not respond, I went to the next one. Nothing. I moved onto the next one. Nothing. The next one, nothing. I became like a desperate gambler at the slot machines in Vegas who moves on when one machine doesn't bring forth a jackpot. This experience was the same as being in a casino and hoping luck was on my side.

I took one final round staring at each individual concrete creation. Standing as still as them, I raised my voice, "WHERE IS MY HOLY JACKPOT?!" They still did not respond, after a few moments of annoyed silence…I heard Kenny Rogers, "know when to walk away and know when to run..."

I looked to the sky with the sun shining through the clouds, where I believed God lived and thought maybe I was supposed to be looking beyond the statues, or at the way the light shined down. Would I see something in the massive heavenly sunbeams or puffy passing clouds? The longer I gazed up, over and around, the more distant God felt. I showed up for my miracle, but he did not produce.

I was disappointed, but not surprised, and honestly a little relieved as the clouds had multiplied eliminating the warmth of the sun. I was getting cold, which made me hope for the burning bush Moses got, perhaps in the form of a campfire, which I would have greatly appreciated as I was turning stone cold like the circle of brotherhood encamping me.

I finally got my sign when I realized that I was not a "chosen one" who God wanted to include in his short list of special experiences. I accepted that and moved on. I left Maria Stein Shrine and all the relics, medals, statues, dead body parts, trinkets, candles, and various tchotchkes with the full knowledge that I was not good enough for God.

8

"You want what for Christmas?"

My Mother

As often as possible and within radio frequency, I listened to preachers throughout the work week emphatically repeat bible verses on every broadcast. Promising it to be *the* most important book we will ever own, describing it as the living, breathing word of God, and our guidebook to life with solutions to any problem now or in the future. They encouraged us to read it to our children, read it with our spouse, with friends, and in the morning, noon, and night. Furthermore, attend a bible-based church. Really?! Was it all that?

They were highly educated, and as if they were real medical doctors, prescribed the bible as the ultimate tonic to all ailments. I followed their advice by listening to their interpretations of the bible and trusted their knowledge.

Even with perfect attendance at church, the Catholics who I know are not readers of the Holy Word. The only bible in my home growing up was safely tucked away in my mother's dresser drawer. It became known to me one day when I was about ten years old, home alone, and snooping around in her room. I looked in her dresser and found a cedar box shaped like an oversized encyclopedia hidden amongst her supply of panty hose.

The box was heavier than my young arms expected, and almost dropped on my foot. I opened the tiny metal clasp to find out what was hidden and discovered a thick white leather book with gold lettering in the center, "The Holy Bible." As I gently lifted it out of the box to open it, the binding cracked as if it had never been opened before.

The pages were thinner than layers of puff pastry, almost transparent, and my clumsy hands quivered out of fear of tearing them. The sides of the pages were a shimmering gold, requiring extra care when handling. It was like finding a buried treasure without the monetary value. Reading some of the words, it looked like a foreign language with sentences beginning with Thee, Thy, and Thou, none of which made sense.

Returning the heavy yet fragile item unharmed back to its hiding place, I never thought about it again, until every preacher and teacher on Christian radio would not stop talking about it. One afternoon a new preacher channeled his way through the airwaves, who was oddly enough talking about the bible in the Catholic religion. He explained how Catholic doctrine and leaders of the church, including popes, bishops and priests forbid lay people to read the bible. He said it was reserved only for the ordained who were qualified to read and interpret the Word for the congregation. Which explained why my mom kept it hidden.

Since I did not recall it referenced in mass or read in my home, it was not something that mattered to me, besides, it was written by a bunch of men 2,000 years ago. Of course, it was not going to make sense or be pertinent in contemporary times, especially to an educated, modern day, working mother like myself.

However, the preachers on the radio made the stories and the people relatable and applicable to everyday issues. They quoted and referenced it in a way that inspired me. The more I listened, the more I wanted my own bible to find the answers and words of wisdom they referenced, and the magic of perfect faith.

The dichotomy between the Catholic religion and other Christian religions regarding reading the bible weighed on my mind. After a little research, I found out that it was true that the Catholic leadership forbade the congregation from reading it, but the plot thickens.

It's important to consider interpretations of foreign languages, the lack of an industrial printing press, and how most of the population didn't read or understand Hebrew. Even though this was the practice long ago, most Catholics today still don't prioritize reading it on their own. My conclusion: there is more to the convoluted and controversial story than I have time to investigate. Plus, it is a book and I believe we are all free to read any book we choose and never be told otherwise.

I thought about it, and kept thinking about it, but never bought one of my own. While working with a colleague one day and riding together in my car, we started talking about various radio channels. I confessed to listening to Christian music and certain preachers who were more motivational speakers than religious people, and how they promoted reading the bible. His head snapped toward me from the passenger seat, his eyes bulged, and his face lit up, he said, "Absolutely, they are right!"

He asked me if I had one, I shook my head no. He suggested a Ryrie Study Bible written in the New American Standard because of its simplicity to understand, and a concordance in the back with definitions, maps, and organized detailed explanations on each page. He thought I would find it easy to follow and promised it would change my life.

I thought, "Who knew?!" Never in a million years would I have guessed *he* read the bible. Why? Because he had a reputation for being a manipulative snake and a liar. I assumed people who read the bible were upstanding, trustworthy, and honest people. Perhaps he had not read it cover to cover yet.

Because of the endorsement of multiple radio ministries and a less than perfect colleague, I was intrigued enough to want one for myself. Christmas was coming soon, and I thought it made perfect sense to share my gift idea with my mother who had been requesting my Christmas wish list. The next time she asked for suggestions, I told her a bible. She said, "What?! You want what for Christmas, a bible? Are you sure you do not want a purse? I picked out a cute one for your sister. I can get one for you too."

It was hard to explain, and frankly it did not make sense to me either. However, the radio programs were making sense and feeding my spirit with each sermon and song, and I wanted more of that feeling. But I did not share all that with my mom because listening to non-Catholic people was frowned upon by devout Catholics. In their eyes, there are only two religions, Catholic and Protestant (they blame Martin Luther for that split), and one is right, and the other is wrong. I didn't know how my parents would feel about it, I did know it wasn't necessary to discuss. My desire and the path that led up to this request was outside the Catholic norm and had the potential for controversy and conflict, and I avoid both at all costs, so the motivation behind my wish list remained confidential.

Ignoring her confusion, I requested the Ryrie Study version. Her hesitation and tone in her voice carried over the phone line from four hours away, knowing full well there would be a purse under the tree and not a holy book.

A few days after our conversation, my mom called to clarify my gift request, "You know that's not a Catholic one?" Admittedly, I did not know there were denominational versions. My assumption was that all bibles were of the same Christian faith. I asked her what's the difference and does it matter? She couldn't explain if a difference existed. I suggested she talk with the priest at the church where she had been the secretary for the last 20 years. If he had an opinion, I was opened to hear it.

Another few days later my mom called, "I talked to Father Dan about it." She paused, and reluctantly said, "He said it was a good version and... (it was a struggle for her to say this) ... a good idea for Christmas. But I looked at the Catholic bookstore and they do not carry that one. We need to find a Christian bookstore to buy it." I heard my dad in the background say, "We have to go to one of those holy-roller stores to get it." I thanked her for checking with Father Dan and left it at that, confident they would not go out of their Catholic comfort zone to make this purchase.

9

"In order to be irreplaceable, one must always be different."

Coco Chanel
Designer

Jump to Christmas Eve, my mother handed me my present, a box a little larger than shirt sized. I fully expected that purse or pajamas or a sweater, but it was too heavy. When I opened it, my jaw dropped, and my eyes widened. It was The Ryrie Study Bible, in the New American Standard language. I was shocked out of my socks, on many levels. One, because she bought it for me, two she got the exact one I requested, and three how excited I was to get it!

My excitement was quickly dulled by the lack of enthusiasm from others in the room. This gift certainly was not as fabulous as a new purse or tool or toy. No one made eye contact with me. Were they afraid I would start preaching? Obviously, this Holy Night was not congruent with the gift of the Holy Word.

Tuning out their lack-luster response, I opened it in search of certain scriptures referenced on the radio, flipping from one delicate page to another. I made sure it had all the bells and whistles my colleague promised, including definitions in the back, explanations on each page and in a language I understood. Yet in the chaos of Christmas wrapping paper being tossed across the room and people tearing into boxes, it was not making sense, so I put it away to enjoy later when home alone.

I was, and still am, a veracious reader, but never anything about church or God or religious stuff. I loved romance novels, true crime or suspense stories, or movie star biographies, but never a Jesus book. But life felt different now and I was different. The romances and mysteries were too predictable and being an overworked, exhausted mother, I fell asleep two sentences into any book. My desire at this point in my life was to read about the stories and people referenced on Christian radio.

The holidays were filled with activities, and I did not get to read my new book for another few weeks. One night with a moment to myself, I cradled it in my dish water dry hands and held my breath while opening the pages, hoping to hear from God. The binding cracked as with any new, hardbound book. Flipping through a few pages, I read some words, then a few more random pages. I checked out the concordance in the back and perused the index in the beginning, but it was still foreign to me. My excitement waned, disappointment filled my quiet moment as I was not able to understand anything I read.

I wondered, "Where are those stories? Where is David and Goliath, Jonah, Moses, the good Samaritan, the lady by the well and the woman who was almost stoned? Where is the dancing David?" My heart wanted to get it, but my mind was not having it. Since I was not smart enough to comprehend the ancient wisdom while conscious, I placed the book on my nightstand hoping the sacred subjects would enter my brain through osmosis while I slept.

I tried over the next few months to read it, get it and memorize certain verses, but it was a struggle. Nothing was changing for the better, nor was anyone speaking to me through it. No divine wisdom mysteriously emanated from the thin pages enlightening my mind. Without much success, I searched for positive sentences like the ones in The Power of Positive Thinking and/or referenced by the radio religious. Locating a few of them sustained me, but it felt like I had only a few pieces to an incomplete 1,000-piece puzzle I should have requested a Catholic version or more practical...a purse.

A few months later, while at a district meeting, I talked with one of my colleagues, Lydia, about religion. She was quiet, genuinely nice and either extremely calm or totally disinterested; the more I got to know her, the less I was sure of which one it was. I cannot remember how our conversation started or the exact topic, but as we talked and walked down the hallway, she told me she was thinking about starting her own bible study. As soon as the words left her mouth, I invited myself. Some might say that was rude; I call it taking initiative.

She was different from the rest of the district. She was humble with her product knowledge and the way she delivered her sales pitch with a softness and genuine intellect, made anyone buy whatever she was selling. And her bright, beautiful smile broke down every gatekeeper's guard. She was the exact opposite of me. When she and I walked through an airport, or a busy area with a crowd of people, heads turned, and people stared at her as if she was America's Next Top Model. She was, and still is, that stunningly beautiful.

I wanted what she had, again not able to name "it," so if she was leading a bible study, I wanted to join. As soon as my self invitation left my mouth, her pace halted as if she hit a wall, she raised one eyebrow, totally taken aback, her radiant smile immediately replaced with a look of regret for letting her thoughts leave her head. Then she clarified with raw honesty, "I did not tell you about it so you would come."

I was not offended in the least. She had something special, and I wanted it too. Accepting her non-invitation invitation, I asked her when it was. She just looked at me. She ran out of space to pull her head farther back on the top of her neck. She paused, her hesitation made me question if it was possible she did not like me personally? We had a good professional relationship, but some people prefer to keep their private and professional life separate. Whatever was in her pretty head and behind her calm demeanor, she did not share with me.

In the middle of asking her about the specifics of the study, another colleague interrupted and ended our conversation. Seizing the opportunity, Lydia turned and walked away without giving me the place and time of her private class. I thought it was an odd response since it was a "religious" study, and once again I expected people who knew the "living word" to act a certain way. Was she a snob, or was I out of line for asking?

I wondered if this was another secret society like priests who consider themselves the only ones "qualified" to read the ancient book and speak to God on our behalf. It was obvious that these religious people do not want someone like me to know what they know. Either way, I was determined to find out the logistics of her private study.

10

"A picture is worth a thousand words."

Fred Barnard
Illustrator, Artist

Lydia, my ever calm and composed colleague, never mentioned the study again. I begged for more details, yet my pleas fell on deaf ears. I relinquished the pursuit and instead relied on the radio for my spiritual lessons. Clearly, their knowledge exceeded hers since they held doctorate degrees in theology. The more scripture I heard, the more I wondered about the Catholic vs non-Catholic versions. There was a Christian bookstore in a nearby plaza that also housed a sports bar, bank, gun store and a medical lab for blood and drug testing. I thought this might be a good place to discover the answer.

I was a little hesitant, not being a frequent shopper of religious stores or ever having the desire to purchase anything religious, except for baptism, First Communion or Confirmation gifts. My reluctance came from a previous indelible experience at the Catholic gift store farther down the street next to the stale bread thrift store.

That vivid encounter began when I walked in and the woman behind the counter remained stationary and on high alert. Nary a smile or friendly greeting to me as I entered the store, but she was quick to ask with intense suspicion, "Can I help you?"

Her social skills resembled the typical church etiquette. I told the lone salesclerk that I was looking for a First Communion gift. Curtly she asked if I was Catholic, which was odd, I was in a Catholic store

43

buying a First Communion gift. Of course, I was. And why would she need clarification before helping me find an item? I nodded my head with affirmation. She sighed with relief, reading the confused look on my face. She explained, "You know there are people who hate Catholics, and my store has been vandalized multiple times out of hatred and discrimination."

I wondered silently, "What is she talking about and who are these people who don't like us?!" I wanted to know more, but she seemed a little on edge and I was not sure if she was telling the whole truth or was perhaps, a little paranoid. My gut said not to question or encourage her and look around on my own.

She continued on her soapbox without giving me any guidance regarding my shopping needs, saying, "It's true, people say we are a cult and are Mary worshipers and the KKK hate us."

I just wanted a First Communion trinket. She continued to explain the history of anti-Catholicism and put us in the same category of prejudice experienced by Jewish people and African Americans. Through her rant, I bought a Precious Moments cross because it was closest to me and I was able to pay and escape before going down a propaganda rabbit hole.

That was my point of reference for a religious bookstore. Imagine my concern going into a Christian bookstore, not knowing what to expect, especially with the volatility of Catholicism. I entered the store with the appropriate level of apprehension. For a small store, it offered a large variety of home decor, books, music, bibles, knickknacks, T-shirts, and jewelry. It was the spiritual version of a Hallmark store.

The friendly male clerk approached, offering his help. I asked him where the bibles were. He ushered me to the back of the store. My eyes grew three sizes as I took in the sight of more than 100 of them. Who knew?! There were leather ones, hardcovered, pocket size, all colors, some for studying, some gender specific, red letters and children's options. And each one had its own sort of Dewey Decimal acronym system with NASB, KJV, NKJV, NIV, REB, NCV, NLT, NIRV, etc.

Without thinking and in a daze of amazement, I inquired about the differences specifically between Catholic and non-Catholic ones. He casually explained, "There are seven extra books or sections in the Catholic versions versus the Protestant ones. They are called the Apocrypha or Deuterocanonical and are found between the Old and New Testaments." I had no idea what those two words meant, Aprocri and deuter what? Moreso, did the Catholics add the extra sections or did the Protestants remove them? The mystery continues.

As I pondered, he explained they offer a historical reference. I appreciated the brief explanation, and since I am not a history buff, the difference seemed irrelevant to me. He further explained that each translation was just a personal preference for a specific language style, study preference, and interpretation.

Maybe I had the wrong version to fit my personality, that would explain my inability to understand mine. Considering my colleague who recommended my version was a snake; perhaps he was misleading me with an ultra-confusing version. My parents should thank me for being so specific in my request and saving them from figuring all this out.

I told the clerk about mine, and he said that was a good one. That made me feel better, but only for a hot minute. Obviously, there was no reason why I should not be able to comprehend it. After he gave me the information I was seeking, I turned to leave the store. Along my path was the wall art section near the front of the store, and something caught my eye, a series of photographs with sheet music within a frame.

My attention focused on one with a black metal frame about 20"x 24" with a black and white "5x7" photograph of a small group of people having church service in what looked like somewhere hot and poor, possibly Africa. Upon closer inspection, the floor was dirt and there were no glass windows, only square openings in the cement walls. No pews, only planks of plywood on cinder blocks, and nothing else.

It was the total opposite of any church I had attended. What caught my attention were the people who appeared to be singing with joy, their faith evident in the facial expressions. There were a handful of men, women, and a few children of all ages and sizes dressed in their best cool cotton clothes.

It was captivating, the extreme contrast from the architecturally designed and grandiose churches I knew compared to their meager church structure. Our churches were opulent with elongated stained-glass windows, gold embossed paintings of the saints, intricately carved wooden Stations of the Cross and hand painted murals that covered ceilings and walls painted by world renown artists. Most of them had life-size statues, some made of marble, of Mary, Joseph, various saints, and enormous crucifixes with a suffering Jesus - items required to create sacred ground.

None of that existed in this church. Nothing. They had nothing. Yet the sacredness of their worship was captured on their faces. It was baffling, "How can they be having a spiritual service surrounded by dirt, fresh air, and sunshine?" The sun shined through every opening in the building onto these people who were holding hands and expressing an internal joy and their visceral experience was captured in a photograph. At first glance, I only saw how poor and pathetic their "church" building was, then I realized it was the fulfilment of their soul and not the physical attributes of the building that mattered more.

How could these people be so happy when they clearly had no money or marble floors or magnificent, gold embossed relics? The song sheet below the photograph was "Amazing Grace," one of my favorite hymns. I quietly sang the words to myself, mesmerized by the dichotomy in the photo as if it were a Picasso playing with my mind.

Something nudged me to buy it, but I didn't listen. It was Christmas season, and better to focus my purchases on gifts for other people.

The impression of that photograph lasted in my mind for days, causing me to question my lack of inner joy when in church, and what makes a space acceptable for worship? Was opulence and grandeur necessary? Those people did not need it. Looking around at others during the typical Mass, most appear bored, and blank-faced, very few reveal expressions of a happy soul.

Deep in my thoughts, "The Grinch Who Stole Christmas" came to mind, the part when he realized Christmas did not come from the store. And I considered faith may not come from a building after all, perhaps church meant a little bit more. The contrast continued to occupy my thoughts. So much so that a few days later I returned to the store to buy the piece of provocative art.

As it hung in my living room, I starred at it for as long as possible, contemplating why this mattered to me and how could I experience the same joy they expressed.

This particular year, I offered to host a holiday dinner party for my district of 10 coworkers after one of our meetings. Typically, we dine at a posh restaurant to enjoy the whole kit and caboodle at the company's expense, from appetizers, bottles of wine, multiple courses, desserts, and being served by bow-tied staff. We treated ourselves like royalty, and for some odd reason, I had the idea that it would be more festive and special if they all came to my house for a homemade feast.

My cooking skills were decent, having parties was fun, and festive cocktails were my specialty, most often with ice cream and liquor. My boss agreed and gave me the go ahead to host. He suggested catering the main course and I accepted the offer to lighten my hostess load.

Allow me to clarify, as much as I loved having people over to my home, the heavy lift of cleaning and making it presentable for guests, was a different story. I prefer a spotless and organized house, but the process of making that happen and maintaining it was not my forte. Cleaning was done on an as-needed basis only, usually for guests and holidays.

My husband shook his head when I told him I invited my district over for dinner because he was aware of making our house "guest" worthy and how much those situations pushed me over the edge leading up to the occasion. The enormous effort to hide school backpacks, homework papers, mounds of mail, dozens of shoes, and balls of every sport turned me into a raving lunatic. My repeated demands to clean up every nook and cranny were delivered with a pitch high enough to make a dog howl.

However, I rally when needed, and was ready for the evening event before leaving the house that morning after days of proper planning, preparing, and problem-solving.

After the typical chaos of getting the kids fed and bathed, I was ready to appear as the ultimate working mother, great cook with a clean house, and perfect family by the first ring of the doorbell. When my coworkers arrived, I greeted each one with an inviting smile and warm welcome to our picture perfect holiday home.

Everyone mingled over appetizers while I excitedly concocted my signature cocktail Christmas drink, which was a mix of vanilla ice cream, peppermint schnapps, and half-n-half in a blender, poured into a goblet prepared with grenadine swirled around the inside, topped with whipped cream, red and green sprinkles, and a miniature candy cane hooked on the side. It was simple and festive.

It turns out, the guys only wanted beer and two colleagues did not drink alcohol at all. Who doesn't drink alcohol at a party? I explained it was not hard liquor, and it did not even taste like alcohol, it was more like a dessert, so why would they not drink it? I pressed for an answer, but they did not offer an explanation other than a half-smile and head shaking "no, thanks."

Being Irish Catholic, alcohol is a staple at every event, from baptisms to wakes, and every gathering in between. Not drinking for this festive occasion was absurd.

The two non-drinkers, one being Lydia, accepted glasses of pop and then walked through my living room talking quietly to each other. Both were genuinely nice people, quiet in nature, pleasant, and always kind. I was busy being a host, making sure everyone had drinks, socializing, and the meal was prepared and served with Martha Stewart style perfection.

While I made my way through the guests in my home, I overheard Lydia and the other soda-drinking colleague talking softly as they stood examining my Amazing Grace picture. Lydia whispered, and they both laughed in a secret sharing moment. I tried to listen to the rest of what they were saying, but their voices became too quiet, and I did not want them to know I was eavesdropping.

The following day at the end of the district meeting, Lydia mentioned the bible study she was starting, and with only slight hesitation, shared with me the details of when and where.

11

"Sailors on a becalmed sea, we sense the stirring of a breeze."

Carl Sagan
Author, Poet, Scientist of the cosmos

The following month the study was to commence. And soon came *the* night to make a horrific fool of myself. All day, questions flooded through my mind, trying to grasp the reasons for inviting myself to a colleague's home whom I barely knew, and who initially did not want me in her private group.

Logic told me the driving force was to discover motivational quotes and develop unshakable faith, the kind promised by the radio preachers. Once that happened, life would be good.

We were meeting at Lydia's house after dinner, which meant getting home by 4:30 p.m., feed my family by 6:00 p.m., and be out the door by 6:30 p.m. The best part of every workday was coming home to reconnect with my children. Leaving them after being gone all day wore on me like a lead apron. Granted my children were in school and/or daycare all day but going out or doing anything in the evening or weekends without them was not something I did. After starting a family, I rarely went out with girlfriends. My husband and I barely went out as a couple or with other couples and I never went on a "girls' trip" like other women.

Time with my children was and continues to be the most important part of my life. I never tired of being with them. Some women did a happy dance when their children went back to school in the fall. My reaction was the opposite, crying as they climbed on the bus another year older, another year closer to growing up and moving out.

But tonight, was different. I assumed God would approve of me leaving my family to spend a few hours with "His Holy Word," as referenced on the radio. Secretly, I hoped to earn extra credit for taking personal and precious time during the week to do something to raise my level of religiousness.

After preparing dinner, feeding the family, and rushing to eat my own meal, I quickly tied my shoes, and my husband asked, "Where are you going?" I shook my head in frustration and explained, "I told you; tonight is bible study at Lydia's house. It starts at 7 and she lives a half hour away, I have to leave now, or I will be late." He shook his head as he looked around at the kitchen to be cleaned and the impending exhaustive bedtime ritual. Our adrenaline rushed at the same level, but for different reasons.

It pulled at my heart to leave my family at the dinner table, but going to Lydia's pulled a little harder at my soul. Coat on, bible in hand, I kissed my disgruntled husband and sweet children goodbye.

The entire drive over I kept asking myself, "Why am I doing this?" My nerves were on high alert. It was a visceral response through my whole body created in my mind that caused my stomach to flip flop with butterflies. It was exactly how I felt when I was a child getting ready for my first dance class. I used to dance around our house every waking hour and begged my mom to register me for classes. But, when the time came for the formal dance lessons, I lay on the kitchen floor curled in a nervous ball refusing to leave the house.

My mom did not force me to go that night, nor any other night thereafter, nor did she register me for another dance lesson. Looking back, I could high kick myself in the butt for not going, because I realized in college what an amazing dancer I was with natural talent and incredible rhythm. This fact was confirmed by my intuitive modern dance professor and anyone who watched me at nightclubs and weddings.

Those little-girl jitters, fearing the unknown, and that feeling of making a complete fool of myself made my heart pump faster with every turn of my tires.

My hands slipped off the steering wheel from nervous sweat escalated by the chatter in my head, "You don't know anything about the bible. What do you expect to be different because of this? You are not a priest or a nun. Why is it so important that you know this?" Countering my self-talk with promises from the radio reminding me, "God's word is the way He speaks to us." And I wanted to hear from God and needed divine direction to be a better person. My life was full of frustration with my job, and my inability to be that perfect wife and mom.

Of course, I kept picturing my children at the kitchen table finishing their dinner and I felt horrible for leaving them with my mothering duties incomplete. I hoped they understood one of the reasons for doing this was to make me a better mother. But who was I fooling? I worked outside of the home all day; I could never be the better mother.

I considered turning around and going home, then "The Power of Positive Thinking" came to mind and a few quotes like "I can do all things through Christ who strengthens me" came back to mind, keeping my car driving towards Lydia's condo, my nerves neutralized. My hope was that this study would teach me the secret of knowing God and answer my lifelong question, how to get into heaven.

After pulling into Lydia's condo complex and finding her address, I hesitated and stayed in my parked car. I wanted to go in, but I did not want to go in. This battle going on between my head and heart was at a standstill and I could not understand either side. After a mental ping-pong game, I got out of the car and methodically stepped one foot at a time with the pace of a snail, approaching the front door, wondering with every step forward "What in the hell am I doing?!"

When I neared the white front door, there were no voices or sounds one would expect to hear from a classroom. It was right at the start of the 7 p.m. hour. Was this the correct address? I knocked gently. There was no answer. That was my sign. Run! My feet did not listen to my brain, and they remained in place as if the cement hardened under my shoes.

In that moment, I hoped I had the wrong condo. I would explain to Lydia how I tried to attend her class but wrote down the wrong address. Now I know what it means to be "saved." This mistaken location would save me from embarrassing myself in front of these religious scholars.

The message from my brain to raise my finger and push the doorbell happened in a millisecond. My hand was like a puppet on a string and someone else was controlling my action. It had been happening all night, from wanting to be there, to driving 30 minutes from home, to walking up the front walkway, to ringing the doorbell. It was my body and my mind, yet my actions were controlled by an outside force or maybe from within, not sure.

I was jolted out of my mental banter when Lydia opened the door. Her reserved enthusiasm and forced smile reminded me once again that I was not technically invited and everything in me wanted to turn around and run back to my car. However, my feet, acting on their own, decided to walk farther into her condo.

I did not see anyone else at first, and a feeling of panic intensified my upset stomach. Am I the only student? This will be impossible to hide in a crowd of two, me being one of them. Two steps forward around the corner into the kitchen, my nerves settled like sifting sand when I saw two other people.

Lydia introduced me to Rhonda, who was about 5'9" with long straight brown hair which framed her strikingly beautiful face mixed with black and brown Polynesian ethnicity. Her make-up was bold with blue eye shadow over her bright green eyes and pink lips. Her body was that of a malnourished runway model with perfectly shaped and highly positioned boobs accentuated by her tight white T-shirt.

Her girls were saying hello to me with more enthusiasm than Lydia. Being eye level with her chest, I could not help but notice. I never understood how a woman could be so skinny in the waist and yet have excessive fat deposits in all the other right places. Whenever I lost weight my chest and butt flattened, resembling a stick of gum from the side.

Next, I was introduced to Amanda, and she was equally beautiful. She appeared to be more Brazilian with long dark, silky brown hair, deep brown eyes, olive skin and a very warm and welcoming bright smile with perfect teeth. She was also tall, wearing stylish clothes and genuinely friendly. Not that Rhonda and Lydia were not friendly, they were more reserved or maybe skeptical of me (those were my feelings, not sure what they were really thinking).

All three of these women were at least 10 years younger than me, not married, no children and looked as if they were here for a photo shoot on the cover of a fashion magazine, and not a religious occasion. Confused and anxious, I thought, "I have nothing in common with any of these women. I am short, three sizes larger, wearing mom jeans and dinner stained t-shirt, pale and clueless with scripture."

Miraculously, my first epiphany occurred: "They do not know me so I can pretend to suddenly get sick or one of my kids is not feeling well and leave early." My GI system responded in-kind with a wave of mouth watering nausea, everything in me knew this was going to be awful.

Lydia had a few snacks on the table, some nuts, a few veggies, and pretzels. Thankfully, some food to ease my nervous stomach. We made small talk and they explained how each of them knew Lydia. They both dated men who knew Lydia's boyfriend. It was comforting to learn that Amanda and Rhonda did not know each other either. Our common thread was Lydia, and to my little knowledge that was our only common thread.

Lydia corralled us from standing around the kitchen table over to the living room. I sat on one end of the full-sized, light blue couch with Amanda on the other end. Lydia took the dark blue club chair and Rhonda was perched on a flowered love seat.

My heart beat against my sternum as we sat down. There was no way I could hide my ignorance in this small group. In classroom situations, it is best for me to blend in with other nonparticipants. I disliked being called on by teachers, professors, or bosses. I never raised my hand to offer an answer to a question, even when I knew the answer. Hiding in a large classroom was easy, but not in a class of three. I asked if anyone else was coming and Lydia said no. Great, I was certain to be the class dunce. It was too late to escape now. Decision made: I will get through this night and never come back.

12

*"Touch the earth, speak of love, walk
on common ground."*

Steven Van Zandt
Singer, Songwriter, Musician,
Producer, Actor, Activist

Lydia started the evening with a few logistics, first and foremost we would start promptly at 7:00 p.m., keep it to one hour, follow a study guide, read scripture, pray and be done on time. She began with a casual and personal prayer. It felt odd praying in someone's living room. The only time I prayed outside of church was grace before meals in the privacy of our own home.

But you know, "when in Rome…" We bowed our heads and closed our eyes and she started, "Heavenly Father, we come together tonight to study your word, to understand who you are and who we are as your children. We thank you for bringing us together, Rhonda, Amanda, Lori, and me. Lord, you have opened our hearts to want to know you and we just ask that YOU be with us. Come into our hearts and help us learn and be changed by your holy presence. In Jesus' name we pray. Amen."

Simple and to the point. She talked to God as if he was a friend sitting on the ottoman in front of her. Does she not know how far away God really is, and what made her qualified to state what she expected of him?! Then she dropped a bomb that each of us will be leading the group in prayer, starting next week. That snapped my head back with a look of 'Oh, no I won't!' She countered my look with an attitude of 'Oh, YES you will.' Unbeknownst to her, there was not going to be a next time; I was not coming back. Public embarrassment averted.

She handed each of us a booklet. It was written by one of the familiar radio preachers. That was a good sign. After opening the first page, we started immediately with an exercise: list three people we knew and three people we knew of. Lydia gave us a few minutes to complete the first assignment.

My list included classic movie stars as those I knew of and my family as people I knew. This exercise gave me pause to consider the slight difference in wording but huge differences on my lists. Prepared to share my easy and safe response with the group, she did not ask us to share. Hopefully, the rest of the night went the same.

Lydia explained, "Notice the difference between the two lists and what makes them different. Think about this. We all know of God, but I want us to know Him with the same intimacy as the people you said you knew. It's about a relationship, a close personal, intimate relationship with God that we will be studying."

Then, she asked us to open our bibles and turn to a scripture of John with some numbers. Not knowing exactly where to find it, I began my search assuming it was in alphabetical order. Not so. In a bit of confusion, I flipped through multiple pages of the supersized book. Yet, no matter where I turned, front to back and back again, I could not find the scripture. I was lost right out of the gate; how hard can it be to find John?!

I noticed a slight breeze through the room accompanying the sound of pages being tossed to and fro. I looked up to see the other two students rapidly searching their books, front to back, back to front, creating a gentle wind through Lydia's living room. Well, well, I may not be the dunce of the class after all.

Lydia, who found her place immediately, sat in confusion at the flurry along her couches. Her jaw hung a little lower, looking puzzled, quietly asked, "Who has never read a bible?" Answer: all three of us. I did have something in common with the other students.

Lydia froze, contemplative, and confused (now we all had something in common). After a long pause, she explained how she grew up in a home where the bible was and is the center of their lives. She humbly admitted this was her first time to host a study. She participated in ones almost her whole life, but never led one. The pregnant pause held all of us in silence, she was flabbergasted by the fact that none of us ever read it, that little fact never occurred to her.

She regrouped her thoughts and told us where and how to find the specific scripture. She distributed crayon-like highlighters made specifically for thin paper and told us to highlight the verse. My hand hesitated. I felt like a real rebel going against centuries of ancestors forbidden to even read this book, and doing it with a group of non-Catholics outside of a Catholic church, and then defacing sacred property like a graffiti artist, blurred the boundaries of my comfort zone.

Everyone else highlighted without concern. Out of peer pressure, I did the same, but barely touching the page with the crayon. Ugh, everything in me felt naughty. Visions of nuns rushed into my head, rulers at the ready to smack my knuckles, followed by a swarm of clergy looking downward through their noses at me in great disgust.

Lydia wrapped up the night early after some brief conversation and resetting our lesson plans to meet the needs of novices. She created a safe atmosphere where questions were welcome, but it was too soon to come to any major conclusions. When it was over, I was glad to have gone, and left energized by the group's positive vibe.

When I returned home, my happy helium balloon popped. No, it exploded. No, I exploded! The kitchen was a mess, plates still sat on the table, pots and pans covered the counter and stove, even more dishes piled in the sink, every child still awake and in need of a bath.

I was not three steps in the house when I lost my mind. I was gone for two hours, and my husband could not take care of the kitchen and kids while I was getting religious. A surge of stress hormones raged through my righteous self, starting at the top of my Rocky Mountain high, to the bottom of the Big Valley below, all in zero to three seconds.

It was not my best example of mothering. I was ultra-angry at my husband, but of course I did not express my thoughts and instead spewed my aggravation on my children. I yelled at them as I hastily cleaned them before forcing them to bed. No bedtime stories. My focus was the pile of work in the kitchen that should have been done, but was not done, and could have been done, that I was now doing.

Why?! Why could he not take care of the children and kitchen this one night? My blood boiled; joy evaporated like steam. I clanged and banged every dish, pot and pan until the kitchen was cleaned. I continued to yell at the giggling kids for not falling asleep as I pleaded with them to quiet down multiple times. I was a flaming hot arrow shooting around the house cleaning up, anger building inside. I second-guessed my decision about going to Lydia's, if this mess and aggravation awaited me upon my return, it was not worth it.

After a good night's sleep, making it through the rest of the work week, listening to encouraging Christian music, I started to look forward to going back to Lydia's. I did not consider the first session to be a real "study," since we barely read anything, or completed a formal lesson or homework.

The next time, before I left, I made sure the kids were fed and the kitchen was clean. I accepted they would be up when I got home. Going to Lydia's was out of the ordinary and I embraced the extraordinary. This was genuinely something I wanted to do. If I were to be selfish and take time away from my family, I must first take care of my real responsibilities as a mother and homemaker. Only then could I be guilt-free and good to go.

The second night of class, I experienced the same excitement and nervousness, still unsure of the driving force behind my desire. There were no major or minor epiphanies at the first one, however the women were pleasant, and secretly I enjoyed the time doing something for myself.

We continued to meet for several months, and during that time we learned to pray out loud with comfort, discussed simple, yet profound concepts and dove deep into scriptures. Sometimes it was only one word, the explanation and context of that word was more meaningful than I would ever have perceived on my own. Lydia had that gift to help novices understand. It was exciting.

The more I learned, the more I wanted to learn. It was like dating a great guy for the first time when I could not get enough of him and wanted to spend as much time as possible getting to know every detail about him. It was the same feeling learning about Jesus and God, who was feeling less distant than I previously thought.

I hold Lydia responsible for that. She summoned the Almighty to her living room with her prayers, like a holy séance. She told us that where two or more are gathered in His name, God was present. I looked around to see signs of a divine presence and wondered if God heard us and saw us or just listened to our conversations. I hoped he was taking notes on me being a star pupil and being involved with this group. The bigger question, would it get me days, if not weeks, out of purgatory?

13

"St. Bernard, calling St. Bernard, you are needed, Code Brown first floor!"

Code for Missing Person in Hospital

Lydia and I were in the same sales role with similar territories and often spoke of how challenging it was to call on hospitals. We were empathetic to the pain and suffering of severely ill patients being pushed in wheelchairs through cold and chemical aroma hallways by exhausted loved ones. The fear of terminal illnesses was palpable, especially so at children's hospitals.

We often complained of the rigors regarding vender protocol for access. The process usually began at the pharmacy, which was most often located in the underbelly of the building near the trash and delivery area. We would sign in, receive an official badge, and then meet with physicians at their office, usually at the complete opposite end of the hospital.

I called on a certain children's hospital numerous times and had a good rapport with the woman in the pharmacy at the sign-in desk. She reminded me of Blair, the cheerleader type character in "The Facts of Life" TV show, with the big head of blonde hair and bright smile with toothpaste ad teeth.

I recall one afternoon when I arrived, she seemed a little irritated. As I approached the counter, she was on the phone with a serious look on her face. I respected her privacy, and out of consideration to her conversation, I stepped to the far side of the counter. While waiting, I noticed the wall of her cubicle was decorated with mass cards of various saints, a small plastic crucifix, a miniature porcelain statue of Mary, a rosary, and medals hanging from silver necklaces.

When her call ended, I commented on how much I liked one of her Jesus trading cards, the one where he had tousled brown hair, a free flowing beard, and soft smile. He looked more like a real person than the suffering one hanging from a cross. She half smiled and said thank you, quickly issuing my badge. No small talk today. My next attempt to engage her was complimenting her Mary statue. That softened her attitude a little. She apologized and said she was in a hurry today to get her work done and leave on time.

I asked if she had special plans for the night. She said "Yes, I do, and we are short staffed around here. I need to leave by 4:30 sharp." Then she asked me, "Are you Catholic?" With the obvious Catholic trinkets, I felt safe to acknowledge my allegiance and nodded my head yes. Then she confided, "Father Leo is coming over for dinner tonight. Do you know Father Leo from St. Joseph's church?" I shook my head no.

She looked shocked, then took a deep breath, closed her eyes and she put her hand over her heart and exclaimed, "He is a true holy man." Opening her eyes, she expressed, "He is so holy that he speaks to our Lord. He is extremely knowledgeable; you know Catholicism is the one true religion. He told me all about it, it is in the bible. There is no other religion recognized by God. Father Leo would know because he has extensively studied it, he is considered a scholar." She kept a posture of reverence the whole time she spoke of him. Her face lit up while she thought of her extraordinary dinner guest.

I promised to keep my visit short and not make her late for her momentous evening. I was curious, though, about the medals hanging around her cubicle and asked who they were. She got serious, looked over her shoulders and around the room, then whispered those are St. Bernard medals. She softly explained, "They keep away evil people."

Catholics have a saint for everything, St. Anthony helps us find lost things, St. Francis of Assisi is the saint of animals, St. Joseph looks after the family (and helps sells houses if you plant him in the yard), and everyone knows about St. Patrick. But who was St. Bernard?

Recognizing the confusion on my face, she continued, "We were having trouble with a neighbor kid. He was bullying my son, he was awful, he physically hurt my son and his mother was even worse. I planted several St. Bernard medals all around the perimeter of our yard. And you know what? A few days later, they put a For Sale sign in their yard and moved shortly thereafter."

She drew closer to me and whispered, "I also put them around this office. There used to be a strong negative vibe in here, because of one woman. She and I battled over religion every day. She was Baptist and caused constant strife in our department. She was rude, manipulative, and a backstabber. It was a very hostile work environment; she ruined it for everyone. I called upon St. Bernard. One day before she came into work, I secretly taped the medals over her office door, under her chair and desk. She had no clue. I put them in our employee break room, by the copier and the coffee pot, and guess what?! She no longer works here." I thought, that explains the short staff.

As odd as she seemed, I thought there was something to those medals. Was it the actual medal or the power of the saint, or both or neither, or was she a Wiccan!?

On my way home that afternoon, I stopped by our local library to check out a book about the saints. Who are they, how many more are there that I do not know about, do they really have special powers and how can I tap into that?

The quantity of books in the religious section far exceeded my energy to search for saints. Not having any detective persistence within me, I had half a mind to return to my car. The other half of my mind spoke up and told my feet to find the Catholic section. My body responded and soon I was perusing multiple shelves stocked with books on saints. I let out an emphatic sigh followed by eye rolls like when someone wants a one-word answer and gets a lengthy dissertation instead.

I love to read, but not too many pages, and this section seemed to have encyclopedia- length books. Where was the pocket size brochure on St. Bernard and the other saints needed to change my life?

I scanned multiple bios of various saints, and briefly looked through a few books devoted to individual saints. I concluded they were all regular people with ordinary circumstances who allowed their faith to set them apart by a decision they made to follow God or stand up for God or have a vision of God or Mary.

I read that scholars were unable to prove the actual existence of some of these saints. I started to question if I should be calling upon a person who may or may not have existed. It sounded more like folklore. Was there special power in that? Granted, there were some with documented horrific circumstances and torture who never wavered in their faith and died for their religious devotion, which is powerful and impressive. I checked out one book that had the most saints listed with the smallest description of each.

That evening I read through the book and discovered.

St. Peter for longevity

St. Christopher for travel

St. Lydwina for skaters (did not specify ice, in-line, or roller derby -they certainly need a saint watching over that aggressive behavior)

St. Elizabeth of Hungry for in-law problems (I am sure she is called upon 24/7)

St. Margaret of Cortona for despairing prostitutes (aren't all prostitutes despairing)

St. Bibiana for epilepsy, headaches, insanity, and hangovers (why are those conditions lumped together?)

St. Zita for people stressed out by household chores – where has she been my whole life?! I need her more than all the others combined.

I kept reading and discovered some were fictitious. Was that the same as fake or "based on a true story" half-truth? I read that St. Maria Goretti, the patron saint of girls, was twelve years old when she fought off a local boy in Italy. He stabbed her, she died the next day, and is honored by the church for preferring death to defilement. I questioned, "Does self-defense or being murdered equal sainthood?" Was there more to the story? Not in this book.

I could not wait to ask Lydia's opinion at the next study session. I wanted to ask before class, so this one time I arrived 10 minutes ahead of schedule. I rushed through her front door as soon as she opened it. I did not explain why or about my experience at the children's hospital. I went right into my question, "What about saints?" Without hesitation, she said, "Do you mean dead people?" And the look on her face told me, 'We are not going there.'

While Lydia didn't want to go there, my mind did. So, in the weeks to come I thought about the saints and their role in my beliefs. Through many discussions with myself, I didn't come to any solid conclusion because I desperately needed extra, powerful reinforcements helping me through this life. My Irish ancestry pulled me in the direction of calling out to every Celtic cousin near and far, in real life or in folklore, especially since my birthday falls on one of the key dates on the Celtic calendar of seasons.

I gleaned much from Lydia's religious wisdom, even though we came from different branches of Christianity. I strongly believe it is important to listen to the interpretation and beliefs of others. I am not threatened by other's opinions, what concerned me was that I might be missing something significant or that I was doing something that put me on a slip-n-slide to hell.

14

*"New beginnings are often disguised
as painful endings..."*

LaoTzu
Writer, Philosopher

I was a work in progress. Week after week, time with Lydia was changing me from the inside. Our lessons always on point, including scriptures specific to being a wife, mother, and working woman. I had no idea the details God was concerned about in my life. When I learned that grumbling and complaining mattered to God, it transformed my attitude. Even more enlightening were our discussions about gossip, the Trinity, worry, and fear.

Some of the most poignant and life-changing scriptures we studied were the ones about anti-anxiety and trusting God with and for everything. One was Matthew 6:25-34 NAS, "For this reason I say to you, do not be worried about your life...do not worry about tomorrow; for tomorrow will care for itself. Each day has enough trouble of its own."

In my Ryrie Bible Study version, that passage was in red letters, which meant they were spoken by Jesus. Jesus explained we are as valuable to God as the animals and flowers which the divine nature takes care of, therefore, and most certainly God will take care of humans. Our confidence comes from knowing the Divine knows everything we need.

Repeating and meditating upon that one scripture comforted my worrisome mind. No matter what happens on this earth, God will care about me and my situation, and know exactly what I need. Learning this was easy; living it was a little more challenging.

It was scriptures, pertaining specifically to trusting in a higher power, that transformed my thought process and broke the chains of an anxious personality inherited from ancestors who lived Murphy's Law of expecting worse case scenarios.

I was on a spiritual roll and loved the thrill ride. It was everything I hoped it would be, conversations within a safe zone and Q & A every week. This was the place where I felt closest to the divine. There was a unique presence with us in Lydia's condo, a peaceful presence, an encouraging spirit. If this were church, I would eagerly attend every day with enthusiasm instead of dread and duty once a week.

Imagine the shock and disappointment when Lydia shared with our sacred circle, gathered for another soul-enriching evening, that she was moving to Chicago. Our time together had come to an end. I felt as if I had hit a brick wall at rapid speed. She received a promotion at work, and she was excited to be closer to her parents. She cut my umbilical cord with her words and removed my heart, soul, and spirit in one swift and very painful snip. She was totally fine with this decision. I was ripped to pieces.

I was just getting to understand God, Jesus, the bible and what it really meant to have faith. She was *the one* who helped make sense of God's word, ways, and wisdom. She was the vessel, my gifted teacher, my direct dial to the Almighty Father.

My heart deflated. I felt abandoned on the side of a desolate backroad during the intense mid-day heat. No one would ever come along to give me what she had given me. My soul was set free because of her wisdom of all things religious. And not only that, her peaceful personality and gentle teaching, along with her example of turning to and trusting in God for everything would be gone. My spiritual growth nipped in the bud before it had a chance to blossom.

She led us through our final lesson and prayer with Matthew 28:19-20 NAS being the launch pad for moving forward without her, "Go therefore and make disciples of all the nations, baptizing them in the name of the Father, and the Son and the Holy Spirit, teaching them to observe all that I have commanded you, and lo, I am with you always, even to the end of the age." We highlighted the verse, letting the words sink into our hearts and relate to the time when Jesus handed the baton to his disciples and how Lydia was doing the same with us.

She saw our long faces and reassured us with multiple scriptures to write down for references and future study. She was confident in our progress and God's presence to take us deeper in our faith.

I felt like one of those disciples in the Last Supper. It was our last night with our Rabbi, our leader, our source of wisdom. It was a feeling of abandonment, a flashback to fifth grade when my favorite teacher, Mrs. Bennis, left halfway through the school year to have a baby. Class was never the same. The replacement teacher could never compare to the original.

Lydia tied up our lesson like a neat little package wrapped with a bow, but all I could think about was never experiencing the word of God again with such understanding. Unable to hold back my disappointment, I begged her not to go. But her decision was made, nothing I said, nor any amount of pleading changed her mind.

Driving home, deeply disappointed and feeling cast aside, I forced myself to conjure up some words of encouragement and repeated "God is with me always." I cried and contemplated her abrupt exit out of my life. I was angry with God too. Why would God take her away from me, just as I was just learning the truth and growing exponentially.

Negative thoughts crisscrossed through my cranium, including the possibility that I was getting too close to the tree of knowledge like Eve when she ate the apple. My spiritual growth was off the charts. With Lydia's one selfish decision, the solid ground crumbled out from under me and was moving to Chicago.

This made no sense, maybe it was not God putting the kibosh on my development, maybe, it was the devil moving her to Chicago and just like with Job, God told the Devil I was up for the taking. Lydia told us the devil was real and extremely active in this world and had an evil army of his own. I have no idea why God allows evil angels to roam the earth and wreak havoc on good people either. That was a deeper thought for another day. Right now, my main concern was me and how to keep my holiness whole.

When I came home, the kitchen was a mess, and the kids and my husband were tangled up in a wrestling match laughing and having fun.

Considering the blunt trauma to my spirit I just received, I erupted like Mt. Vesuvius and I let every person under that roof feel the wrath of my wounded soul. How dare he play around when the kitchen was a mess, homework unfinished, and kids needed bathed?! My anger was completely redirected at my children, when again it was meant for my husband, and tonight for Lydia and God.

Once again I flipped on my kids when they had nothing to do with the circumstances causing my aggravation. They had nothing to do with Lydia leaving or unfinished housework or getting themselves ready for bed. Those were my jobs and I failed, all because of going to a bible study where it ended without finishing the study guide. My spirit was cut down like a freshly planted tree bearing its first buds. My poor children. My unfortunate husband. Welcome one and all to my pity party.

Later, I flopped into bed, and took a few deep breaths after tossing and turning to get comfortable. Once I settled, my soul reminded me of the biblical story we recently studied. The one about Martha and her sister Mary who were hosting a special guest, Jesus. Martha was the worker bee consumed with making sure everything was perfectly in place to accommodate the traveler. Mary spent time listening to and being in the presence and perfect peace of Jesus. An angry and bold Martha complained to Jesus about her sister's lack of sharing the duties and told him to tell her to help. Imagine the audacity she had to complain to and nag Jesus about her own sister.

Then Jesus told her, "...you are worried and bothered about so many things, but only one thing is necessary. For Mary has chosen the good part..." (Luke 10:38-42, NAS).

My husband choose the good part, spending time playing with, laughing with, and being in the presence of our children. I was Martha, he was Mary. Lord help us both.

Many days later; an epiphany. Maybe, just maybe, God thought I relied too much on Lydia and my reverence and dependence were on her and not on the Divine. Not sure if that was true, but it allowed my heart to soften a tad, refocus on scriptures trusting in God's plans, and open to finding another Lydia.

15

"You've got to do your own growing, no matter how tall your grandfather was."

Irish Proverb

I needed to find another Lydia, and fast, before I lost momentum. The only way my spiritual self was going to survive and thrive was to find another study group led by a woman who knew the bible with the same knowledge and humble personality as Lydia. Equally important was finding the right church and denomination to honor the Sabbath. Therein started my simple and secret quest. Keeping it hush-hush avoided conflict with the devout Catholics in my life who believed it was a sin to attend a church outside the "faith."

The Catholic church with its abuse scandal and cover up, false teachings, and exclusivity of women in leadership went against my spiritual grain. I believe those issues are a greater sin than me attending a different denomination. The challenge of enduring mass was amplified when priests performed the ceremonial aspects with repetitive boredom and coldness. Cut from the same cloth, the organist used the same dull musical score and tempo for every song and the choir was borderline pathetic. Music should add to the worship and not make me cringe or want to pull my hair out one strand at a time.

Music in the church was important to my dad too. He believed the whole mass experience was elevated with talented musicians and vocalists. On occasion, our church choir expanded by adding a few extra instruments making it the "contemporary" mass. When my parents attended those services, afterward my dad expressed how pretty the flute or violin sounded, never mentioning the forgettable sermons. He would have loved for Eddie Arnold or Tammy Wynette to lead our choir.

Since that never happened, he expected whoever led the choir and congregation to hold a tune, a fair expectation. We agreed on the importance of vocal quality and additional instruments to enhance the musical experience. Where my dad and I differed was our expression of our dislike for the music. I would shake my head and keep my irritation suppressed, but my dad was more publicly expressive than I, and a union man.

One organist hired by his home church, the place who employed my mother as their secretary, did not possess a good singing voice. She had a talent for playing an organ, but somewhere along the line someone should have encouraged her to pursue a non-vocalist career. It was a unanimous dislike among the parishioners, some shared their opinions with the pastor, who they knew held the power to hire and fire her. But being a man of the cloth, he kept her in place hoping to grow the fruit of mercy and grace among the hearing abled staff and lay people.

She was the organist for a few years, then one weekend my dad's frustration peaked, and he did what any hot-headed Irishman with a union card would do: he picketed. He made a large sign that read "Fire the Organist" and he stood outside church at multiple masses picketing the organist and getting signatures of support to get her fired. That was my father - a man of action to right a wrong.

My actions were a little more subtle. My decision was to attend a Black Catholic church to improve the music and energy. I was hopeful there would be a passionate, quality choir as I considered the pop stars who sang in their church - Aretha Franklin, Whitney Houston, Otis Reading, Marvin Gaye (imagine Amazing Grace sung by the singer of "Sexual Healing"), and Donna Summer – disco in the church – that would keep me in the pew until the final note was sung. Attending a Black church would meet my need for a soulful musical experience while keeping my obligation to my family and religion, and significantly increase my chance of finding my next Lydia.

One Sunday without notice, I told my family we were going to a different church, St. Joseph, in downtown Cincinnati. There was some resistance to the extended car ride, but our children weren't old enough to fight me, I still had "Mom" power. We walked into the church and were greeted with spoken salutations and bright smiles; the atmosphere was that of an ice cream social. Parishioners were hospitable to all who walked in, there was mingling and conversation amidst the aisles, pews, and even near the altar.

Arriving to a social atmosphere gave me hope that I found the right church combination of inspiration and spirit-moving music. I was correct on one thing: the choir had heart, talent, and movement. The style of the mass altered in a few ways. The congregation was much more expressive throughout the whole service, some saying "Amen" and other words of affirmation out loud and throughout the priest's homily. In most Catholic churches, no one raised his/her hand in agreement or ever shouted an AMEN.

This church understood my groove with a relaxed atmosphere, friendly parishioners, freedom of expression from the lay people, and spiritual music. This experience fulfilled my soul's searching.

Unfortunately, the 30-minute commute was an easy obstacle to deter my family and our attendance was short-lived. My search continued.

I explored the closest nondenominational "Christ" church, without my family. Arriving in the lobby with only a few minutes to spare, a quick decision was required between "Traditional Service" or "Contemporary Service." People flowed rapidly through the lobby, and it wasn't clear what the difference was, or which way the majority were headed. In a split-second decision, I followed those surrounding me into the traditional service.

In search of the right seat, no one acknowledged my presence, and that felt familiar. The crowd was older, judging by the sea of grey hair, no young families or children, and people were spread out as if threatened by a communicable disease.

As I walked down the center aisle, my attempts to make eye contact to join their pew failed row after row. Every person stared straight ahead as if mannequins. Being ignored happened over and over and by the time I ran out of people to look at, I was in the front row.

The organist played what could have been the soundtrack to a horror film. People were silent and stiff with a chilling vibe. I was ready to leave as quickly as I arrived, but too embarrassed to walk out prematurely.

On the flip side, the sermon deserved "three and a half stars" for the middle-aged preacher man with greasy black hair dressed in a business suit with cowboy boots. Looking past his persona, his message hooked me when he spoke about appropriate versus inappropriate anger, starting with driving situations. Like me, he cannot display a Jesus bumper sticker on his motor vehicle.

He recalled his parents arguing with voices loud enough to be heard in the next county, and it frightened him as a child. He wasn't ashamed to admit his personal struggle to appropriately express rage, and quickly transitioned to mention the good kind of anger that brings about needed change, including civil rights and working conditions. As good as the sermon was, this was not the place for me.

16

"It isn't what you do, it's how you do it."

John Wooden
Basketball Coach

Next on my test drive, the local Presbyterian Church, the place where my neighbors attended. I knew they would introduce me to their church friends who would be as neighborly as they were to us. I couldn't find them before the service started, so I slid into one of the pews in the very back section, to make an early exit if need be. The goal was to observe the service, including the sermon, quality of music, and overall vibe of those in the pews, and leave unnoticed - all parts of the equation when evaluating an acceptable church.

A senior woman grabbed the open space beside me at the last minute sharing a smile as wide as her head and leaned into the invisible shield of my personal space as she settled in. The expression on her puffy pink-cheeked glow was as if she hit her mark and I was the target. The person at the altar welcomed everyone and requested newcomers fill out the cards provided in the pew with our contact information. The woman handed me the card, I politely declined since the purpose for my presence was observation only, no follow-up required.

Refusing my polite decline of the card, she pushed the index card closer to my hand. I shook my head and kindly stated, "No thank you, I'm just visiting." She assumed I lacked the understanding of the purpose of the card and explained how the church likes to know who is visiting. Through my shy, forced smile, I politely shook my head "no."

My focus remained on evaluating the flow of the service, music, and getting something out of the sermon. As the choir began and my ears perked, she noted I wasn't holding the hymnal or singing. No one has ever labeled me a vocalist. Even though I deeply appreciate the powerful experience of music through rhythm, lyrics, and a fun beat, I refuse to sing out loud. Unless, I am alone in my car, or at a concert or dance club where the volume far exceeds my off key singing.

As with any good movie, the music accompanied our next struggle. She pushed the hymnal in front of me to get the words out of my mouth. Her attempt was unsuccessful and only fueled her fire. I focused forward and enjoyed the pleasant voices filling the walls of worship. Her growing frustration presented her with a dilemma, unless one is a trained ventriloquist, it's near impossible to purse your lips and sing at the same time. She started breathing deeply and loudly through her nostrils.

She continued to force the hymnal in my face hoping to bring a song out of this bird, not so, my beak closed tighter. The poor dear was no match for my stubbornness.

To her dismay, I wasn't playing her game, no matter how hard she tried throughout the service. She persisted with her agenda to the very end when she wouldn't move out of the way for me to leave the pew. The sore loser of her own game offered a fake farewell, "I pray you find what you are looking for." If she's the example of how this church operates, no thank you, I won't be back here either.

The next church experience came out of the blue when my daughter played basketball in a Christian league where the rules included equal playing time for every player. No superstar favorites, no coaching for the win, and not even a score keeper. It was all about giving every player a fair chance, the opposite of when my children played sports in the Catholic league where some children sat the bench the entire season regardless of never missing a practice or game. In that league, I witnessed some of the worst behavior from coaches toward children, young children just learning a sport. Appalling.

At the end of my daughter's season all the players, coaches, and families were invited to a banquet/church service at the Nazarene church. We went as a family to support my daughter.

This service began with a jolt, blaring contemporary Christian music with a live band as if attending a rock concert. A complete band with a piano, full drum set, guitars, keyboard, saxophone, trumpet, trombones, violin, flute, and organ (which was drowned out by the rest of the instruments), and the best vocalists I've ever heard in church. They sounded exactly like the songs on the radio, or close enough for me.

The first five minutes were visceral from the vibrations under me, within me, and all around me. I was unable to control my feet from tapping and hands from clapping along with the crowd. And with the music the decibel of a jet engine, I sang out loud.

They invited all the basketball players to join them in the nearby gym connected by a long hallway to the main church. At the doorway between the hall and the church they had set up an archway of balloons and streamers and played pre-game energizing music as loud as an NBA arena. I was mesmerized by the flashing laser lights crisscrossing back and forth, and a fog machine! It was a major production as they introduced every player by name and the whole church applauded as if these children were superstars. The kids loved it, the parents loved it, and the congregation loved it. I have never been so pumped up and jazzed within church walls ever, and I fell in love with all of it.

The sermon was engaging and inspiring by the pastor, who was also one of the basketball referees. He was funny, natural, personable, and an excellent orator. Toastmasters would hail him as king. The prayers were genuine and heartfelt, prompting "AMENs" out loud by many, and I felt my hand almost raise once in praise and worship. But I behaved, refrained, and stayed calm, yet in awe, and did not let anyone around me sense the Holy Spirit doing jumping jacks inside my soul. This was the church experience I longed for, and I could not wait to go back again.

17

*"Life is not about waiting for the storm to pass...
it's learning to dance in the rain."*

Vivian Greene
Artist, Author, Entrepreneur

Months and years came and went, the Nazarene service was everything I'd hoped for, and I attended as often as possible, but I was alone in my connection to the service. Dividing the family for church attendance didn't sit well with me and to keep peace, we remained faithful to the Catholic church. It wasn't "the perfect church" for me, and thought, perhaps if I became more involved it would fill the void. That led me to teach Sunday school, volunteer as a lector, serve as a Eucharistic minister and join the health and wellness committee.

At this time, I learned we really did read scripture during mass. The first reading is from the Old Testament, the second reading is from the New Testament, and the gospel, the reading by the priest before his homily, is from one of the four gospels of Matthew, Mark, Luke, or John. All these years, I just thought they were random stories.

Even with my extra involvement, church was still not moving my soul the way that studying the bible, or the Nazarene experience did. I kept listening to Christian radio, read daily devotionals, and spent mornings in quiet prayer, but never found another Lydia to lead and teach me. We did, however, keep in touch over the phone, as I called her frequently with biblical questions and life issues. She never disappointed and continued to willingly share heavenly wisdom with grace and kindness.

On Saturday, April 22, 2006, around 11 p.m. during a pop-up thunderstorm with quick flashes of lightning and a steady crack of thunder, I finished watching a movie in my bedroom. Then I caught a few minutes of the news to see if the storm would be severe or just move through the area. There were only a few red spots on the radar, and I told myself, it was nothing significant and will pass over, and fell asleep.

One hour later our bed shook, and a flash of light lit up the room, as if an M80 exploded outside our window. The near explosion set me straight up. I immediately thought we were under attack and hit by an enemy bomb. I jumped out of bed, just missing my daughter who was asleep on the floor beside me and undisturbed by the sound. My husband's slumber was disturbed, briefly, and he quickly fell back to sleep.

I went into the hallway where my one son came out of his room, and another up from the basement, and realized there was no electricity to investigate the situation. The only clue was the pounding rain with pops of lightning and roaring thunder.

The smoke alarms began their high pitched and steady beep, but we had no idea why. The constant alarming sound finally forced my husband out of bed to join our search, or so I assumed. He thought it was an electrical power surge and went around to disconnect each smoke alarm trying to turn them off, to no avail.

Then we started to smell burning plastic. We awakened everyone else and congregated by the front door concerned about what to do and still unsure of what was going on. Then, from my son's bedroom on the second floor, smoke slowly swirled out the door like a snake on the move.

We immediately ran out the front door and into my husband's Ford Expedition in the driveway. I called 9-1-1 on my flip cell phone and then got out of the vehicle and stood in the rain talking to the 9-1-1 operator staring in disbelief at my house. I explained what happened and she said help was on the way but kept me on the phone asking for more details.

Then I heard them…the sirens…they were faint at first, then became louder and louder the closer they raced to our house. When I realized those sirens were en route to help us, the alarming noise comforted my nerves. It was the calvary rushing to rescue us; it was simultaneously exciting and soothing.

As soon as the first police officer arrived, he went inside the front door, but quickly ran back out as the whole house was filled with smoke. Then the fire trucks and rescue squads started arriving along with every neighbor on the block and all three television news crews. There were four different fire departments and 20 various emergency vehicles at the height of fighting the fire, according to our neighbor who counted. It turned out that our home and several houses on the street were hit by lightning. The storm continued with intermittent rain, thunder, and lightning.

The firemen could not locate the source of the fire, and at one point, the fire chief, who was standing in our driveway, lost communication with the firemen inside our house. We stood helpless as they hacked the roof and busted in the back door. With their hoses winding through the front door, fire personnel circled the perimeter of our house and across the roof.

All we could do was stand outside in the rain watching and giving thanks that we escaped safely. Our younger children went inside the neighbor's home, while my older sons stood around with friends their age and several neighbors who gathered to check on us. We stood beside each other, wet from the rain, unable to move as we watched and waited for the fire to get worse or be extinguished. My husband and I answered interrogating questions by the fire chief.

The scene proved surreal, watching smoke pour from the roof, windows, and the front door, wondering about the fate of our life's accumulations, family pictures, money, everything we owned. Was it all destroyed? The firemen took shifts going into our home, circling the yard, talking, walking back and forth, the smoke did not stop moving either. The rain slowed and the storm ended as quickly as it began. That small red blip on the weather radar turned out to be something not so insignificant after all.

Once the fire was satisfactorily extinguished, the police department roped off the house with "the tape," the neon yellow "DO NOT CROSS" crime scene tape. My gut winced. Suddenly our situation went from a house fire to a crime scene. We were told the state fire inspector would be out the next day to determine the exact cause of the fire.

I asked if I could go back in and get my purse and some medications. The chief agreed, but made us wear their gear, official fire department hard hats and jackets. Escorted by the chief, my husband and I retrieved a few items. He led us with a heavy-duty, rescue strength flashlight into the dark, lung-pinching smoky air with water dripping everywhere. After finding my purse among the waterlogged wreckage, I retrieved my bible.

The house was a disaster. Smoky soot covered every surface with a thick layer of grey heavy dust, water saturated furniture, carpet was soaked and squished under our feet with each step, and puddles covered the hardwood floor. Insulation dangled from the ceiling and littered the floors amongst the broken glass near the back door, along with holes in the roof and walls. The kids' bookbags, shoes, clothes, toys, leftover Easter candy and fake grass from their baskets were strewn randomly on the ground. Even though some of it was like that before the fire, I shamelessly blamed the fire department for making the whole mess.

The activity of the night ended around 4 a.m. when the last fire truck drove off and neighbors dispersed. Our family stayed with neighbors that night. The Red Cross offered us a hotel room, but we did not want to leave the neighborhood. I planned to go back into the house after sunrise to get a better look at the damage and find out if our family pictures and other mementos survived in a salvageable state.

As I lay in bed at the neighbor's house across the street, I had a direct view of our home and could not take my eyes off the damaged structure. It was eerily dark inside, with black smoke stains above the front door and windows, and crime scene tape blowing back and forth in the spring winds. A sickening feeling permeated my stomach.

My mind ticked, too alert to sleep. I never experienced anything more traumatic in my life, except when our twins were born 11 weeks early and were given a 40 percent chance of surviving. I thought about that while staring at our house and tears came easily thinking about how lucky we were then and now that everyone was okay. What if our smoke detectors failed? What if we all slept through the loud bang like my youngest son and daughter did? There were three children in that basement when it caught on fire, what if they got trapped? The "what-ifs" and waves of gratitude would not stop tossing about through my mind.

18

"Sympathy is no substitute for action."

David Livingstone
Physician, Missionary, Explorer

The following morning, I awoke before everyone else in the house, slightly on purpose and mostly because my body and mind could not rest. I was overwhelmed with worry about the extent of damage, insurance coverage, so many unknowns and we had nothing but the clothes we wore as we ran out of our burning house. No toothbrush, toothpaste, shampoo, moisturizer, or clean socks. Nothing. It was unsettling; knowing that our life, as we knew it, would never be the same.

The enormity of the situation was too difficult to grasp. Giving up on my attempt to sleep, I left the warm bed where my husband was tossing and turning and picked up my bible to go into the garage for time alone and not disturb the others.

I secured a foldable lounge chair and nestled next to my neighbor's spare refrigerator. Taking a few deep breaths, I knew what my first step needed to be. Numb from the shock of the fire and based on the reaction from our neighbors, we were knee deep into a major crisis.

In solitude, my mind quieted and my heart opened to a feeling deep within that was encouraging me to handle this differently than I, and anyone else, expected of me. I began to see this as an opportunity to put my new level of faith into action. My response facing the destruction of my home had to be one of calm, strength, and hope, especially for my children.

Part of me welcomed the opportunity to prove to myself that my faith really had grown over the last few years, and if it had, then I could show others how a woman of faith acts when faced with a crisis. I was not completely confident my faith would stand up under intense pressure, but everything in me wanted it to show up and show up bigger, stronger, and bolder than I ever imagined possible.

To pre-load my soul before this day of a new normal, I began with opening my bible. The first step had to be reading God's word before talking to anyone or seeing the inside of the house, and definitely prior to making any decisions. I wanted to make certain my faith was secured to face whatever was about to happen.

I held the soft, black leather book in my cold and shaking hands, and said a few prayers of thanksgiving and praise while asking for wisdom. As only a loving God can do, the exact lesson from my daily devotional guide on that exact day was Romans 5:3-6 NAS, "…we exult in our tribulations, knowing that tribulation brings about perseverance, and perseverance, proven character, and proven character, hope; and hope does not disappoint, because the love of God has been poured out within our hearts through the Holy Spirit who was given to us…" a physical wave of calm came over me, the devotional also included Romans 8:28 NAS, "And we know that God causes all things to work together for good to those who love God."

And then the big one from 1 Peter 1:6-7 NAS, "In this you greatly rejoice, even though now for a little while, if necessary, you have been distressed by various trials, so that the proof of your faith, being more precious than gold which is perishable, even though tested BY FIRE, may be found to result in praise and glory and honor at the revelation of Jesus Christ." I marveled at such divine delivery of exactly what I needed to hear when I needed it!

I felt surrounded by a reassuring presence as I read, prayed, and breathed in and exhaled an aura of peace giving me strength and confidence that everything was going to be okay. I could and would rely on God's direction, and trust in whatever awaited us when we stepped into our damaged home. There I was in someone else's garage, sitting in a folding chair next to a family minivan, tools to my left, toys to my right, coolers stacked on top of each other, and a beer fridge as my sacred space. Is this how and where God shows up? How odd, and personal.

My first phone call was to Lydia for biblical reassurance and wisdom. I explained what happened and that I was alone in my neighbor's garage holding my bible. She was horrified to hear about our house fire at first, then thankful we were safe, and moved beyond tears when I told her how I started my day with God's word and seeking spiritual direction. Then she prayed with me.

Once the sun rose and everyone else woke up, we crossed the street to go inside and evaluate the severity of destruction by daylight. We were fortunate to live next door to a fireman. He was our guide as we walked in a state of shock into our incinerated home. Looking at burned walls, stairs, doors, and floors, we stood in the exact spot of the foyer where we had just been hours ago wondering about the loud noise. Now, we could see the open sky through a new hole in the roof. We choked on the thick air left over from the indoor bonfire as we went from room to room to see what was salvageable and what was destroyed.

My knees weakened when I saw the sofa bed in the basement. Next to this bed was where the fire ignited and where my youngest son and his friend were sleeping, my oldest son's room was just beyond where the lighting surged through the basement. I pictured them sleeping as the fire erupted in the utility room between them. They could have been trapped, they could have been severely injured, they could have… died…the rush of evaded catastrophe flooded my mind as we sloshed through every room.

I kept repeating we were extremely fortunate that everyone escaped without harm. Yet seeing my children's handcrafted elementary school artwork and cards half cindered and their dirty handprints on the wall that I never washed off to remind me of their cute little hands, was extremely difficult to process.

We could not stay inside long due to the extensive infrastructure damage and the smoke stinging our airway. The basement stairs proved unstable, the flashlight exposed the charred wood and apparently where the heart of the fire erupted.

My one neighbor drove me to the store to purchase our immediate needs of toiletries, and basic living supplies. Deciding on such items as toothpaste and shampoo seemed trivial, yet vital. I was dumbfounded by the situation and raw with emotions, making these simple decisions became an enormous task. That afternoon, people from all over dropped off clothes, gift cards, offered to make meals, and asked how they could help. Our closest neighbors joined us in our front yard. Some walked through the house to check out the damage, but mostly they just stood with us as they had done through the wee hours of the night.

Another neighbor made a meal of Greek chicken for everyone who had gathered in the driveway and yard. We stood around eating together off paper plates. No one knew what to say. For me, words weren't necessary, their actions said everything. It was the most heartwarming example of neighborly love and support from friends, neighbors, and a few strangers.

The following day we met with the insurance adjustor, whose incident report confirmed our house was hit by lightning. He shared the lightning strike report where it listed our address as a direct hit. The initial investigation claimed that the bolt of lightning struck the copper water pipe and traveled to the utility room in the basement where everything caught on fire.

We took up residence at the local Marriott where the staff, who were aware of our situation, made a basket of goodies for our family and treated us with kindness and compassion. Eventually we moved into a rental home, with rented furniture, rented beds, rented sheets, rented pillows, and with rented kitchen supplies. Nothing belonged to us.

The days and weeks following the fire were a new level of trauma. They placed an industrial dumpster in our driveway to throw away the damaged contents. The structure of the home was solid, but the entire inside needed restored.

One day, I pulled up to check on the progress and saw our club chair in the dumpster. I stopped in my tracks and stood frozen with memories flashing through my mind. That was the chair where we fed our babies, held toddlers in our arms, cuddled, read books, watched movies, and took naps together. This was so much more than a chair; it was a priceless treasure. And it was upside down in the metal bin like yesterday's trash.

And so it went with many "things" that were full of memories, items irreplaceable because of sentimental value. My middle-school aged kids could not go back to pre-school and make Mother's Day cards with their handprints. It ripped my heart out to throw away those scribbled words "I love you, Mom" in their four-year-old handwriting.

My husband understood the sentimental value of those items and how seriously I take my role as a mom. On the Mother's Day while living a rented and displaced life, my husband gave me one of the most thoughtful gifts, a plate that read, "Home is where the mom is." He was right, being together, wherever that may be, is home. He gets it.

It went from bad to worse when the arrogant and stingy insurance adjuster fought us on every item to be replaced as if it were his money being spent. We hired and fired three incompetent contractors. We fought over every item in our house, from carpet to cabinets to tubs to light fixtures to the brand of paint. Every single item was a constant battle between us and our insurance adjuster and the contractor, one was as shady as the other.

Our insurance company wanted to spend as little money as possible, while the contractors wanted to make as much money as possible, leaving us fully flimflammed.

This went on month after month after month. There were lawyers and lawsuits. Shopping malls were built in less time than it took to restore the inside of our home, which by the way, was never repaired correctly. Our plumbing and electricity never worked the same again.

With every heightened aggravation, I kept on my knees in prayer, trusting the Lord with every idiot we encountered. I was determined to demonstrate to our children how a woman of faith handles trials and tribulations. Some days were easier than others; thankfully God was present and kept me from curling up in the fetal position and crying or going after someone with a hammer. This was not the time for angry outbursts or a pity party, besides what good would it do?

Friends and family inquired, "How are you managing? I do not know how you are doing it. If it were me, I would just sit and cry." I knew that wouldn't solve anything, and it would be a pathetic example for my children. I remained focused on deepening and exercising my faith muscles. If testing was the way to triumph, bring on the exam. When others admired my strength and fortitude, I became stronger and more determined, while my soul knew the real source of my strength.

19

*"A man loves his sweetheart the most, his wife
the best, but his mother the longest."*

Irish Proverb

A year later, with the insurance company refusing to pay anymore for our temporary housing, even though the restoration process was still incomplete, we returned home amongst the disarray. Exhausted from the battle; we were simply happy to be back home.

The time in my car while making sales calls was as therapeutic as medicine. Various preachers and spiritual teachers fed my mind while contemporary Christian music fueled my soul. Perfectly timed praise and worship songs provided the appropriate dose of musical magic, releasing negativity from my body like air out of a Tupperware container. My soul jumped with excitement when I recognized and repeated certain scriptures along with the messages and music. Christian radio and audio books became my mental and emotional lifeline, they were spiritual superfood, especially on the days when I felt like a pig on a stick being roasted over an open fire. My minivan was a church on wheels charging my spiritual battery with positive faithful energy.

Although, on occasion, there would be a sermon on something that made me say "Hmmm." For example, the multiple sermons about women should stay home and be homemakers, was especially hard to digest. Gainfully employed since I was fourteen years old, it was obvious from the start, being single, married, or a mother, one income was never enough.

Admittedly, I questioned if being home 24/7 was the best choice for me. Weeknights, weekends, and holidays were spent cooking, cleaning, grocery shopping, running kids hither and yon, endless errands, and constant yard work. Every minute of every day was consumed with doing something for the house and the people in it. I love my husband and children, and our home, but to only tend to the work of keeping house would not be a good fit for me. Living without my church on wheels Monday through Friday would bring my happy heart to a halt.

That one specific message that never lifted my spirit, in fact added a heavy load of guilt every time it was delivered by multiple male preachers, underscored Proverbs 31. It is the one they declared was biblical evidence for women to stay home and take care of the family as their sole priority. They confidently stated the bible backs this plan for all families. Not wanting to go against God's rules, nor could I quit my job, the daily contention between eternal salvation and financial security fractured my heart.

Having more time with my family to be that mom in charge of the classroom parties and sports team mother, was everything I wanted. However, if it meant standing in my kitchen day after day preparing meals, cleaning up after the meals, then getting ready for the next meal…how was that spending more time with my family? Until I could employ a cleaning service, a fulltime chef and chauffeur, gardener, and handyman, I was working outside the home.

That sermon followed me around like a bad scent, do I stink for not wanting to stay home? Am I going against God by working outside the home? After repeatedly discussing this subject with my husband, he always assured me that working full-time outside the home was needed financially. I trusted his assessment of our finances and kept gainfully employed. Then one day, one life transforming day, something nudged me to look up the scripture the radio Doctors of Theology referenced.

Proverbs 31:10-31 ESV, The Virtuous Wife. After reading it for myself and careful analysis of what she really did in that chapter and verse, EUREKA! She was NOT a stay-at-home mother! Picture this…

"…She seeks wool and flax, and WORKS with willing hands, she is like the merchant ships bringing her food from afar (grocery shopping or farmers market), she gets up while it is still night, provides food (cooks) for her family and servants (cleaning service, chef, chariot driver), she sets about her work vigorously (back breaking), her arms are strong (exercises), she sees that her trading is profitable (smart business woman), her lamp does not go out at night (insomniac or watches late night TV or prepares lunches for the next day), her hand holds the distaff and grasps the spindle with her fingers (she sews), she opens her arms to the poor and extends her hand to the needy (volunteers at the food shelter), when it snows, she has no fear for her household, for all of them are clothed in scarlet (she can afford fancy clothes from Lands' End), she makes coverings for her bed, she is clothed in fine linen and purple (think Martha Stewart), she makes fine linen garments and sells them, and supplies merchants with sashes (Coco Chanel, sales and marketing)…she watches over the affairs of her household and does not eat the bread of idleness (never sits down, naps, or eats a hot meal), …honor her for all that her hands have done, and let her works bring praise (she wins Wife/Mother/Woman of the Year).

There was *no way* anyone, except a patriarchal minded man, could read that scripture and say, "Women should stay home, raise a family, and make housekeeping the joy of their life." She left home to do business. She was a smart successful entrepreneur. She was creative, hardworking, and had a staff of servants. Part of me started to feel inadequate for not working enough compared to her, I did not own my own business, nor leave my warm bed while it was still dark. She was the ultimate over achiever, or was I a slacker? Which triggered another layer of guilt, because being lazy is a sin.

Then something prodded me to read the verses prior to 31:10 and the background from whence it came. It turns out the detailed list of a Proverb's Woman was the criteria from a mother to her unmarried son in the dating scene. King Lemeul's mother begins her suggested list with "an excellent wife who can find?" Excellent question future mother-in-law.

It's obvious, she did not want her son to marry. She knew if she gave him this laundry list to find "the right" woman, he would stay single and her golden boy for the rest of their lives. I was not falling for it anymore. I was not taking what the radio doctor was prescribing. Not today, sir, not today!

Lemeul's mother also told him, "Do not give your strength to women…" Typical head space for a future mother-in-law. Contemplating this scenario about the preface of The Virtuous Woman, I somewhat understand this mother's concern about relationships taking her child's strength. I have known people and relationships throughout my life, and it's true on both sides, with boyfriends and girlfriends, that some people can suck the life out of a person and be all-consuming to the point of toxic.

Even greater transparency, being the mother of three boys, her point of view of wanting the best woman for her son was completely understandable. Prior to my epiphany, I prayed for my sons to get a Proverbs 31 woman as their wife. Which was ironic, because as a wife and mother, I knew full well trying to be that woman was impossible.

The Lord knows I have tried to be her since Day One of my marriage. On one occasion when we were first married, I started to make scalloped potatoes, I opened the box and poured the dehydrated potatoes into the baking dish, as they pinged like pebbles against the glass, my husband asked, "What's that noise?" I said, "It's our dinner potatoes." His response, "My mother never made anything from a box." And that was the last day I ever made box potatoes, or anything else that was not homemade from scratch like his mother.

The day I read the backstory to Proverbs 31, I learned the most important lesson, that when reading scripture and listening to sermons, it is imperative to read for myself the whole passage, and consider the context, time and backstory, and cross reference multiple translations. It was and is the living word of God and if I intended to follow it, then I needed to read the true source for direction and the meaning of every scripture for myself. Decades of guilt lifted away like a hot air balloon rising above the treetops. I was LIBERATED and VALIDATED!

20

"Nothing attracts me like a closed door."

Margaret Bourke-White
Photographer

God's word was my refuge, like the day after the fire, I turned to it immediately for wisdom. I would open the life handbook as soon as any situation arose for the quickest and best advice.

Once after a colleague attempted to slam my reputation within our company, I found peace in 1Peter 3:16-17 NAS, "…and keep a good conscience so that in the thing in which you are slandered, those who revile your good behavior in Christ will be put to shame. For it is better, if God should will it so, that you suffer for doing what is right rather than for doing what is wrong."

Those words silenced my anger toward the colleague's attempt to deface my reputation and allowed me to surrender the situation to God. It was a perfect opportunity to trust in a higher power with a situation beyond my control. The conflict resolved in my favor and without me making a fool of myself.

Another time while stressing out about the holidays and visiting family and friends, I found solace while praying for God's wisdom on handling the impending barrage of criticism. The mystical moment is etched in my memory bank. I was on my knees in our living room, in the corner where I created a little sanctuary of sacred space with candles, angel statues, and rocks or something from nature, leaves, sticks, flowers, etc. And of course, plenty of dust from a working mother with children and dogs to dirty up the place.

I was stressed about the visit because, for anyone with a family and/ or friends knows, there is that "one" person who can ruin the holiday for everyone. I was dreading the criticism about my kids' hair being too long or too short, not the right clothes for the weather, or food issues, the list was endless of what I did wrong. This person's words replayed in my head like a stuck record. I never had a good comeback to stop the ego driven deluge. This particular morning my prayer time was spent pleading for words to stand up for myself. When nothing came soon enough, I started to rise and when I did, I distinctly heard, "let it roll off your back."

I stopped midway to standing and dropped back on my knees. That was not my voice, nor my idea of a good comeback. I requested, "come again, please." Clarifying what I heard, "let it roll off your back?" Really?! Each time I repeated the words, I questioned that wisdom, "you can't be serious, how is that a worthy defense against their judgement of my mothering skills?"

While not agreeing with this notion of simply ignoring the critics, I realized I was questioning divine direction that I had just requested. What was I doing brushing off the very wisdom I begged for?

Recognizing the absurdity of my disagreeable attitude towards the holy cosmos, I accepted the direction and repeated "let it roll off your back" over and over, and half heartedly thanked the divine for answering my plea.

After the visit and on the way back home, I mentally noted the wonderful weekend. Then I remembered my pre-trip prayer preparation and wasn't sure if nothing was said to incite my aggravation or if God covered my ears from their words or held their tongues from speaking. Or had I finally done everything right in their eyes? Whatever happened was by divine design, and it was the best holiday visit to date.

The following year brought on bigger challenges with the economic crash and burn of 2008, when the housing market imploded, investment banks went belly up and the pharmaceutical industry turned upside down and terminated thousands of reps across the country, including me.

I saw it as a gift, an opportunity to pursue my first true love of community health education and physical fitness. It was a tremendous relief to be out of a large corporation where I never really fit in.

Once that chapter closed, I looked for something in health education and exercise. During one of my daily devotions, I was enlightened by 1Corin. 6:19 NAS, "Do you not know that your body is a temple of the Holy Spirit who is in you, whom you have from God, and that you are not your own...glorify God with your body." This was a game changer for my personal health and wellness routine and ignited a fire to help others develop a healthy lifestyle honoring their bodies and therefore honoring God.

My exercise time became an extension of praise and worship as I worked out listening to contemporary Christian music. The combination of an upbeat tempo with spiritual lyrics created an elevated energy, making me unstoppable racing through the streets of town and superhuman strength to lift heavier weights than I did when I was in college. Dancing like David along to praise and worship songs aligned with every cell in my body.

Stretching to a reverential hymn, like Where You Belong by the News Boys, deepened my respect for this temple created to house the holy spirit and drew me to a place I had never been before. Every breath I took, every mile I ran, every weight lifted, elliptical ellipted, bike cycled, and yoga twist was done out of gratitude for the gift of a healthy, vibrant body. Getting spiritually rejuvenated while physically fit was and still is an invincible force in my life.

One day, an ad for an Activities Director at a retirement village in a nearby rural town caught my eye. I was unfamiliar with the area, the facility, and this position, but the job description was intriguing, and my creative mind went wild with how much fun and impact I could have in this leadership role. The ideas filled my head with programs and activities that I would want to participate in if it were me living there - book club, exercise classes, day trips, plays, art shows, etc. I couldn't write fast enough in my notebook to prepare for the interview. My excitement built with every unfolding idea, thinking about how great it would be to bring healthy activities to this special population.

During my interview, I made it crystal clear that if they hired me, I would not lead a group of elders around a card table making childish crafts, nor play bingo or bridge. That was not my expertise, nor desire.

This position was a gamble, I wasn't certain if it would be a good fit for me; older people annoyed me with their slow walking pace, even slower driving skills, and listening to the same stories repeated over and over was mind numbing. It was odd I was pursuing this position with how strongly I felt. However, I was unemployed and wanted to get back into health and physical education. My unexplainable passion for this position was so far out of my comfort zone it should have been a clue that the divine was involved somehow.

They offered me the job the following day, and from day one of employment, it was love at first sight. Every resident I met, every event we planned, and every conversation was filled with genuine connection through mutual respect. The moments of being in their presence listening to their stories nurtured a part of me I didn't know existed. It far exceeded any history lesson read from a book because they told of an event on a personal level with the unique perspective of living it.

Sitting beside any one of them as we conversed over a cup of tea or coffee or punch, brought forth a deep peaceful feeling that I was exactly where I was meant to be. That sense of being in the perfect professional role never existed with any other job and that feeling of purpose energized me like that bunny who never stops beating its drum.

It was also a Christian organization where sharing my faith was encouraged, and the potential for a bible study stirred an internal hope that maybe I would find my next Lydia. To my surprise, I did not find one Lydia, instead the campus was full of Lydias. Countless men and women, who by the way they lived with integrity and kindness to one another were living examples of God's love and mercy.

Their gentleness, patience, and positive encouragement were more inspiring than a hundred sermons. The swimming pool was one of the best places to hear and receive the wisdom of those possessing the benefits of age. I was the instructor of the exercise class and lifeguard, but they were the ones teaching me.

One woman in particular quoted scripture every day. She instinctively knew what I needed to hear, and she was the living example of Titus 2:3-4 NAS, "Older women likewise are to be reverent in their behavior, not malicious gossips, nor enslaved to much wine, teaching what is good, so that they may encourage young women to love their husbands, to love their children…"

The residents asked about my family in a caring way, not nosy, and I would share the latest proud mother moment, or school and sports woes, or the daily dilemma and discord of six people living under one roof. They often laughed and smiled from a heart of understanding and compassion, and then offered sage wisdom to help me through the challenges and blessings of raising a family.

One resident I will never forget was a retired college professor after his career as an engineer in the auto industry. Our friendship cultivated during our time together in pool class, his participation in every event I planned, and his frequent visits to my office where he delivered York Peppermint Patties every Friday. His insight opened my mind to different perspectives, our conversations were lively, thought-provoking, and always humorous.

We laughed at his jokes, and his sense of humor kept me grounded when life upset my apple cart. He brought me a souvenir from one of his many traveling adventures, a little white wooden helicopter. As soon as he saw it, he bought it for me; he was aware of a few of my not-so-proud parenting approaches, and considered me a helicopter mom.

21

*"All people are good. Some just need
a little more help with it than others."*

Marlin Hackney
Wise Elder

Every moment with those senior adults brought unspeakable joy to my soul. I believe it was the ability to see each of them as a valuable individual, still worthy of spending time together, worthy of a smile and to listen to their needs. One man with advanced dementia, who lost most of his ability to speak coherently, knew instinctively that he could trust me and would point to me and tell his aid, "She's nice, she's a good one." They knew I would patiently help them with their TV remote or join their side in the battle for better food, or ensure women kept weekly appointments with the hairdresser.

And their families knew they could always call me, and I would step in and step up for whatever was best for their loved one. Visiting residents when they were in the hospital was exceptionally defining of my care for them and their trust in me, and through these critical life moments I became close with some of their children.

The residents redefined my idea of fun, watching them have a good time, laugh, and develop friendships at this stage in life made my heart sing. Our unique bond went beyond Bingo and Bridge (which I learned to respect, but never played). I felt the pain of losing someone dear and not having enough time together. Meeting some of them in their 90s and 100s, when they passed, I wasn't ready for them to leave this earth, we had so much more to talk about, more history to learn, more wisdom to share, more laughs. Attending funerals and birthday celebrations of bright-minded centurions always gave me pause to consider their journey from the early 1900s to present day.

Two years in, I was promoted to marketing and admissions coordinator. It was a role best suited with my pharmaceutical background and sales experiences, yet I continued participating in some activities with the independent residents. My title changed, but my relationship and heart to serve them never wavered or diminished.

It was during our one-on-one conversations when I knew I had found my calling. They needed someone who would listen, someone who cared, an advocate and a friend. I happily filled that role and will always be eternally grateful for the personal stories and private situations they entrusted to me.

Religious people talk about the fruit of the spirt of Jesus as love, joy, peace, patience, kindness, goodness, gentleness, and self-control. The people in that village showed me and shared those fruits with me daily. As I walked to my office every day in the assisted living hallway, we greeted each other with genuine smiles, our faces lit up since the excitement to see each other was mutual.

It warmed my heart to see couples holding hands as they gently walked everywhere together, balancing each other. Patience and mercy were the cornerstones by which spouses cared for a loved one with Alzheimer's or another debilitating condition that robbed them of their golden years.

I felt the presence of God and the power of the Holy Spirit multiple times a day in every resident's kind words, gentle ways, compassion, forgiveness, and the love...the love overflowed.

I had been doing a daily project for a few years, so that at the end of that year I would have something to look back upon and know I had done something worthwhile. A few daily projects included a photo a day, a Woman of the Day, and a word a day.

Motivated by these residents who found the good in people and joy in their days when their lives were not perfect, I decided to implement a daily project lead by Philippians 4:8-9 NAS, "Finally, brethren, whatever is true, whatever is honorable, whatever is right, whatever is pure, whatever is lovely, whatever is of good repute, if there is any excellence, and if anything worthy of praise, dwell on these things. These things you have learned and received and heard and seen in me, practice these things, and the God of peace will be with you."

This project changed the trajectory of my life, my attitude, and how I handled frustrating situations and irritating imbeciles. Seeing the good in people wasn't instinctual and this project alone cured my negative and judgmental bent.

My job with the senior community never felt like work. I never cared about receiving a paycheck because of how much my life was enriched by serving them in whatever capacity was needed. But eventually paychecks became something worth caring about, and that is why I had to leave my dream job. An old friend from my pharma days reached out and offered me a position with a small biotech company marketing a unique product, including a financial package I could not refuse.

My energy, excitement, and spirit sank as my soul turned to the dark side being led by money. I worried about the welfare and future of the residents. Who would or could replace me? No one. I knew no one could fill my shoes with the same heart, compassion, and level of advocacy as me. One Catholic resident referred to me as Mother Superior because of my fierce protectiveness, fearless leadership, willingness to take charge, and I was Catholic. I became the best version of myself from being around those residents and their families.

I promised the residents that I would do my best to remain in communication with them as I walked away from the one and only job that filled my soul with unprecedented peace and purpose. What's interesting is the place and situation my dad dreaded more than anything, being in a nursing home, was the one place where I found my true calling. Those eight years were the preeminent years of my professional life.

Along came another opportunity to trust God with my next move. Would it be as wonderful as the outcome of when I trusted him with the position at the retirement village? I had no idea how much this change was needed until later.

22

"No man ever steps into the same river twice, for it's not the same river and he's not the same man."

Heraclitus
Greek Philosopher

On June 26, 2017, a day etched in my memory, I drove off in my yellow VW Beetle leaving behind a village full of people I loved, taking with me a mind full of cherished memories, a career that transformed my life, and a pain in my heart so severe I sobbed with every rotation of my tires. Forsaking all that was authentic, kind, respectful and fulfilling to willfully work restrained by golden handcuffs turned my stomach inside out.

I took backroads home passing by the horse farm where I used to stop to take pictures and talk with the horses. I felt a hint of solace looking at these beautiful animals silhouetted in their pasture with the backdrop of an orange sunset. Then my misery worsened upon realizing my daily dose of equine would be no more.

Seeking comfort in my pain, I turned to the airwaves desperately searching for a song to fully commiserate with this momentous loss. I didn't lose one best friend, I lost three hundred of them.

The song on the radio, Tell Your Heart by Danny Gokey, immediately empathized with my situation when he sang of being shattered into a million pieces and experiencing something devastating unlike ever before. I needed this song at this very moment, the timing of when and how God speaks confounds me every time.

I reflected that the job at the village was a situation where I had released the outcome and stepped out in faith to follow a flicker in my heart. Never did I imagine that I would be the recipient of more authentic love than I could ever share with them.

I went into full trust mode when I applied for that position, and never regretted a moment from the start, and on the final day of our time together, it hurt like hell.

I had come to believe that when life was not going my way, keeping my trust and hope in God kept my soul at peace regardless of the situation, surroundings, and outcome. Those moments were slow to recall as I sobbed, blubbering the words as I sang along feeling the fear of making the wrong decision. Even in my sadness, there was a matchstick-sized flame flickering deep within, knowing God cared enough to bless me with eight amazing years with those residents, and to trust in God's presence in this moment on my ride home. Certainly, God will be with me going back into the avarice forces of pharmaceutical sales.

I remembered Lydia explaining to me about Jesus' friends and how desperate and hopeless they were at times. Driving along the two-lane road, tears blurred my vision, and the essence of living in authenticity diminished with every curve. Once home, it was my bible where I sought words of comfort, knowing it would take divine power to rescue me out of my pool of pity.

I found 2 Corinthians 1:8 ESV, "For we were so utterly burdened beyond our strength that we despaired of life itself." Jesus' team suffered, almost to the point of death. I cannot imagine God's best buddies losing hope, and if they did, of course I would too. They experienced far more harrowing situations than leaving an ideal career. They faced physical cruelty, espionage, imprisonment, life-threatening storms, and were ostracized from family and friends.

Under impossible conditions, their faith and trust remained in God's strength, timing, and perfect will. God held them in his hands, and those same loving hands were holding me. I was broken and had no option but to hold onto the stories from God's word promising everything would work out for our good and according to God's perfect plan.

The following six months were a challenging transition, crying throughout most of my days and feeling frustrated with the world. Imagine the let down from being a much-needed resource with a higher purpose for so many of the most wonderful people, to just me in my car, alone and lost looking for clinics with the wrong addresses, wallowing in my sorrow.

Everything in me regretted making this move, but I committed to giving it my best until my children graduated from college. Never could I have known at that time the real reason for leaving the village had nothing to do with money.

At the retirement village, my role was like the center of a wagon wheel, connecting with every aspect of operations including the residents, various departments, families, the community, and outside resources. It was energizing to be needed and work collectively. I took a hard left turn going from sweet, cake-baking elderly folks to irrationally rude gatekeepers and stop signs on physicians' office doors declaring NO REPS. I was not welcome and treated as the enemy.

Podcasts, the library app on my phone, and Christian radio saved my sanity and salvation. I needed to dig deep to find a higher purpose in this role. I found it when I remained focused on selling a product to a vulnerable population that saved lives and positively impacted community health. Moreover, it was an opportunity to exercise my trust muscles, much like after our house fire, and live each moment remembering God promised to never leave me.

During one of my down days, a dear friend and soul sister of mine who understood me better than most suggested that perhaps it was time to look outside my occupation to nourish my soul. She was right, and because of her encouragement I discovered something completely new to me and yet had been with me my whole life, Celtic traditions, history, and spirituality.

I learned prayer, meditation, communing with nature, caring for those in need, hospitality, art, and imagination are cornerstones of their practice. The presence of the spirit is in all experiences, therefore encountering God is in every area of life, especially with the natural world and supernatural forces.

I embraced all that was Celtic, fully immersing myself in the music, meditation, and great outdoors. My genealogy is deep in this region of the world and the spiritual practices felt as natural to me as dancing. The typical personality traits of our beloved Irish and Scottish ancestors include being whimsical, emotional, and great powers of imagination, coupling that with the gift of gab, storytelling, irrepressible buoyancy, vivacious spirit, and kindliness toward frailties of man, personal charm, warmth, and wit – I'm all that and a bag of fish and chips.

It was fascinating to learn the early Celtic religion conflicted with the highly structured Roman church over certain practices. One such difference was the belief in honoring the living and breathing spaces on and of the earth. They believe in angels and the veil between this world and the next is very thin where they experience ancestors and angels frequently. Most important to me is how they recognize and encounter the divine in everything.

The more I read, practiced, and appreciated God in all things, then everything became spiritual and filled my soul unlike ever before. More so than any hum-drum church service.

One cannot walk two feet outside a door without stepping into God's best work and infinite source of life. My morning exercise routine continued to be a time for prayer and praise. The list of people and situations to lift in prayer far exceeded the allotted time for an average workout.

Walking, running, or biking while conversing with the Creator became gratitude journeys where I marveled at being able to see, hear, and smell every object and season under the sun, including the sun itself with its size, warmth, energy, and glorious entrance on the horizon welcoming a new day. Bird's nests left me awestruck as did the various species of trees in which they were built. Holding my sense of awe were cloud formations as they changed and the speed at which they traveled.

My gratitude deepened as my heart opened to divine messages offered through nature. Every person's individuality is likened to the uniqueness of a flower's color, fragrance, size, shape, specific environmental need of soil and sunlight to thrive. I appreciate the reminder of letting life flow while watching a river travel over rocks and fallen tree limbs. There's something soothing and satisfying to the senses listening to the rush of water from the smallest stream to the mightiest ocean. I am further awe-inspired by the infinite life within the microcosm of dirt, forests, and under the sea.

I began to hear God's gentle voice through the summer breeze, a babbling brook, chirping birds, and buzzing bees. Spider webs became works of art created from their body to capture food and were most visible with a dew fall.

This enlightenment was further enhanced after listening to a sermon about God's first creation being nature and the cosmos was the first word and life form, and God said it was good. Reading the scripture for myself and meditating upon the holy concept, my appreciation for divine presence in the great outdoors grew from a seed planted in my mind to a way of being with the vast greatness of God.

Seeing God living and breathing in the outdoors opened my heart and eyes to divine signs and symbols. One day while riding my bike and worrying about my son who was moving five states away to finish college, I was deeply troubled that he would be too far away. What if he got sick or in a car wreck? Or needed help with school or making meals….so many situations when he would need his mother and I wouldn't be there for him.

When I stopped in a random parking lot to catch my breath and drink some water, my eyes turned to the clean black asphalt. There was a feather, a huge grey and black goose feather. Instantly my head and heart connected with God's subtle message that it was time to let my son fly. That wise inner voice said, "let him go, I've got him. Remember, I take care of the birds and lilies and how much more I care about my children, your children, your son."

The exact same thing happened when I was ruminating about my daughter moving into her own apartment near campus. She was leaving my protective bubble to live in the sketchy unknown where she would be coming and going all hours of the day and night, working, going to school, studying, and meeting strangers. Was she ready for that? I was not, so how could she possibly be ready to live outside the security of our home?

At my peak of anxiety, I opened our front door to go on a run and on the front porch lay a little feather, a precious multi-colored white, grey and black feather reminding me once again, it was time for my child to fly and God will protect her just as he always has, and did for my son, and my other sons when they flew the nest.

I've mentioned previously how I assumed God was far off in the clouds somewhere, assuming he was beyond a measurable reach, yet hovering close enough to zap me when I sinned. Imagine my surprise when I discovered years later after reading several scriptures about "clouds" that I wasn't totally off and perhaps I am an Intuitive, someone who knows something without any direct evidence or reasoning process.

God used a cloud according to Exodus 13:21 ESV, "The Lord went before them by day in a pillar of a cloud to lead them along the way…" Did God manifest as a cloud or just ride it like a magic carpet? Then in Luke 21:27 ESV, "And then they will see the Son of Man coming in a cloud with power and great glory." And in Acts 1:9 ESV, "…he was lifted up and a cloud took him out of their sight."

My intuition was correct when I envisioned God in the clouds. If I hadn't discovered Celtic spirituality, or studied the bible myself, I would never have known this.

23

"My flesh and my heart may fail, but God is the strength of my heart and portion forever."

Psalm 73: 26 ESV

"Your dad had a stroke," explained my mom on a voicemail one day in early November 2017 during the middle of a workday. I called her back as soon as I listened to her message. Fortunately, it was not a debilitating stroke, however his primary care physician suggested further testing at the hospital, and when they did, they discovered his carotid artery was 90 percent blocked and required surgery.

The surgery to unclog his artery was scheduled a few days later, which gave me just enough time to take off work and be with my mom and sister at the hospital. The surgery went well and as soon as the anesthesia cleared his mind and body, he asked for a hamburger. He made a full recovery, then a few weeks later started to have some shortness of breath and lung X-rays were ordered to check for potential pneumonia. The radiologist saw something suspicious and suggested more in-depth testing for a definitive diagnosis. He consulted with a pulmonologist who ordered a lung biopsy.

The biopsy was scheduled for early February, and I planned to be there again to support my family. Unfortunately, after celebrating my birthday several days in a row with an impressive quantity of alcoholic beverages, pizza, hamburgers, French fries, charcuterie boards, and desserts, I was admitted to the hospital myself. The attending emergency department physician stated callously that I could die. I requested a more detailed explanation, he said my lipase (a digestive enzyme) was 19,000 U/L and my organs could shut down; normal is 0-160 U/L.

My diagnosis – pancreatitis with a large stone blocking the main duct. Surgery was ordered, I refused, but committed to not drink another drop of alcohol or consume high fat foods ever again and ride it out.

It was good-bye chocolate martinis, adios blackberry sangria, auf wiedersehen Rhinegeist Bubbles Beer. Our time together was wonderful, and like everything else in this life, it had to end. I was a social binge drinker in high school and college, and into my mid-twenties. I am not proud of this; I blame the Irish genes. I was extremely hung over the day of my wedding after imbibing too much wine at the rehearsal dinner and regurgitating in the bathroom most of the morning. How irresponsible of me to wake up on the bathroom floor the day of my nuptials?!

One year later, the alcohol consumption stopped the minute I saw the positive sign on my first pregnancy test. Raising children allowed no time for hangovers or to be without my wits, so I rarely drank anything for the next twenty-five years. It was not until my children were grown when I began to enjoy a glass or two of a variety of alcoholic beverages.

I did not tell my parents right away that I was in the hospital or about my chronic pancreatitis diagnosis. They had enough to worry about with my dad's lung biopsy.

Unfortunately, his biopsy was inconclusive. They put in a temporary tube to drain the fluid following the procedure, and the plan was to monitor his symptoms.

For me, the rest of the month included procedures to remove my stone, making it impossible to travel and see my dad. The month of March was clouded with him not improving, and a new onset of pain in his lower rib cage kept him in bed and unable to eat. Some days he tried to keep active in life, but he struggled. He blamed the drain for being improperly placed. My mom had to drain the fluid frequently which only caused greater distress.

The excruciating pain my father was in coupled with the intense helplessness my mother felt created a horrible ordeal for both my parents. Neither of us could travel to support each other.

The following month my daughter went for some routine lab work to check on a few concerns and to establish baselines with specific health markers. After the blood draw was complete, I chatted with the phlebotomist, and mid-sentence we heard a crash. My daughter fell to the floor, hit her head on the chair and was out cold.

The lab tech told me to push the oversize blue button on the wall. I expected another person to come in and help us get my daughter off the floor. Nope, that was the button for the crash team to respond.

All hell broke loose in that small exam room. At least eight people rushed in with a back board, all kinds of equipment, security, doctors, nurses, social services, administrators. I almost blacked out from the surprise attack of the response team, and all I wanted was to help my daughter.

The dazed and distant look on her face once she opened her eyes scared the life out of me. She looked lost, confused, and her coloring was as white as sterile paper on the exam table, and she wasn't speaking. Fortunately, we were already at Children's Hospital and they knew exactly what to do.

It was horrifying watching your child be strapped to a backboard with a potential back or head injury. I wondered if her condition was worse than I originally assumed. I had no answers, only a sickening feeling. I prayed silently for nothing to be wrong with her, and for me to keep my head straight, nerves calm, and trust she was in God's hands.

She was stable and alert once we got to a room, although still confused about what had happened. The doctor reviewed the lab results, everything was within appropriate ranges, and her vital signs were normal. They assumed she stood up too fast, or possibly not eaten enough since she had to fast for the lab work.

However, when we went for a follow up visit two weeks later, and they took her vital signs again, they became alarmed, ordered an EKG immediately in the exam room and said she was being directly admitted to the hospital. They could not get a reading on the EKG, her weight and heart rate were exceptionally low, and they said if we took her home, she could die. My mind baffled about what was happening.

They admitted her, and continued testing, and involved every department from nutrition, psychology, social services, cardiology, physical therapy, attending pediatricians, medical students, residents, calling themselves her "team."

This went on for three weeks, and every night either her dad or I slept in the chair by her side. This team did not provide a solid explanation for her extended admission. Even though I continued to push for an acceptable diagnosis for their decision, it was to no avail. Once I started making calls to friends who were cardiologists and explained the details of my daughter's physical health, they too questioned the admission.

As soon as I explained to her team that I consulted other clinicians outside their system, they released her that afternoon. If they had not discharged her, I was prepared to break her out AMA (against medical advice).

Being a mother, nothing keeps me on my knees and in prayer more than my children. Especially when they are physically hurting or struggling with life. Thankfully, my sacred morning ritual of prayer, meditation, and reading devotionals sustained me through the whiplash of the highs and lows of parenting. Sometimes the low plateaued with minimal improvement, and I wondered if God really listened as much as I hoped. His lack of answered prayer never stopped my conversations. I prayed out loud when I was alone; we still didn't pray as a couple or a family. However, my silent prayers and conversations with God never ceased.

Between my dad's unmanageable pain, my daughter's hospitalization, my pancreas procedures, we were a hot mess of health hazards. It was a difficult time for our family. The "worry" scale was off the charts with the "what if" scenarios playing out in my head. Was the suspicious spot on my dad's X-ray terminal lung cancer? Was my daughter's condition more serious than the labs revealed? Was my stone possibly pancreatic cancer?

24

"The Spirit Himself testifies with our spirit that we are children of God..."

Romans 8:16 ESV

There's no time like the present when being told death is a possibility to get real with God. Three lives were hanging in the balance, and I was not leaving anything to chance. I dove headfirst into every scripture about healing, printed them out and pasted them all over my home office walls. Some may not believe in the Lord Almighty, but I think their beliefs change when faced with a life or death situation.

I saw this multi-layered trial as another opportunity to trust in all God's promises of healing, "Heal me, O Lord, and I shall be healed" Jeremiah 17:14 NKJV, "For I will restore health to you, and heal you of your wounds, says the Lord." Jer. 30:17 NKJV, and "O Lord, my God, I cried to You, and You healed me." Psalm 30:2 NKJV. I let these words and promises sink into my psyche and soul as I prayed them for the three of us and two friends waging their own war against aggressive cancers.

My pancreas issues were being addressed as best they could, my daughter was moving forward, and I wasn't exactly sure what was going on with my dad.

One day while driving the four-hour trek back to Cincinnati from Evansville, Indiana, I stopped for a coffee and gas break. I phoned my parents to see how my dad was feeling and to give them an update on my daughter and me. Typically, I was not someone who called people just to chat. I phoned if there was something to communicate, but calling just to call was not something I did post teenage years.

Conversations between my parents and me were light, usually about the weather or how family and friends were doing. I would ask what was new in the local newspaper, which did not enrich the conversation much. Most of our time was filled with breathing and small talk, miniature sized conversations described our exchanges. This afternoon proved different with sharing health updates, but even so, I assumed the exchange would be quick and to the point.

My mom answered the phone sounding distressed. My assumption that all was fine vanished, and I asked immediately what was going on. She clipped, "Nothing." But I heard emotion in her voice and pushed, "You sound upset. What's wrong?" She would not elaborate and out of respect, I let it go and moved onto my daughter's health and my good medical reports. Then I heard my dad yelling and carrying on in the background. I asked, "Why is Dad so upset?" She would not explain, so I asked to speak with him.

He said hello and acted fine with me, but I heard agitation in his voice and asked him what was going on. His voice became a little more intense, "Your mother just has to have the glider out of the garage. She is making me move the chair and get everything out on the front porch today. It cannot wait. Everything must be done the minute she asks!"

His rage was a familiar reaction. While growing up, his anger reared its ugly head most during major projects from opening/closing the pool, decorating for Christmas, driving too far in one day on vacation, or when talking back to him. There was no reasoning with him when his Irish was up.

This time was no different as I tried to understand the situation through the phone and calm everyone's emotions. While I only had a snippet of information to go on, it seemed to be a major reaction to a minor situation. I went back and forth between the two trying to figure out what led up to this exaggerated response to moving a glider, all while keeping my nerves in check to be the voice of reason. I was able to de-escalate the situation for the moment, which was probably the first time ever. I must have felt bold and authoritative with a buffer of being on the phone seven hours away.

I hung up, got back into my car, and then I was fired up. Why did my father have to be such a hothead? Why can't he be more patient, cooperative, and calm? Yet if he was in pain, why did my mother insist on moving the stupid glider while he wasn't able to function? I knew all too well how the simple act of moving a glider turned into an argument.

My head replayed memories of my dad's outbursts, leaving the house squealing the tires in a rage over something. It frightened me as a child. He was a great man but look out when he was angry. I didn't want to be a carrier of those genes, but I was, and my own fits of rage joined the movie reel in my mind. I wondered if I scared my children the way my dad's rage scared me.

I recalled one time, out of total frustration, I raised a white Corning Ware casserole dish above my head and smashed it to the hardwood floor with all my motherly might in front of my children. It shattered into pieces like Moses' original Ten Commandments tablet when pushed to his breaking point. People pushed my buttons too, and soon more of my raging lunatic moments came to mind.

With one click of the dial, a song came on the radio reminding me that I am a child of God. I started to cry and reassured myself that indeed I am a child of God. As God's children, we inherit divine character and genes. Yes, I am a child of God. I sang, I cried, I was disappointed in my parent's interaction and with myself for my own outrageous outbursts.

The long drive gave me pause to consider if something more serious was going on with my dad. The next time I spoke with my parents, I offered to go with them to future doctor appointments for a better understanding of his health and exactly what was occurring. His pain was not subsiding and his frustration toward my mother, and even the friendly neighbors, was escalating.

From my work in long-term care, I questioned if he was starting to show signs of dementia or end of life agitation. I was not in town often enough to completely understand his health, the progress of his recovery, or lack thereof and the dynamics of my parent's relationship as they grew older.

My maternal grandparents' relationship drastically morphed when my grandfather had a debilitating stroke, leaving my grandmother with the stressful full-time job of caregiver. I wondered if my parents' relationship was following the same pattern, complete with an exhausted caregiver and a scared and frustrated patient, who didn't want to be sick, incapacitated, and a burden to his loved ones. Their dreams of traveling, and endless conversations relaxing on the front porch faded too quickly.

The day of my father's doctor's appointment, I met my mother, sister, cousin, and my dad at the Cleveland Clinic for a second opinion with a pulmonologist. My dad was sitting in a wheelchair when I met them in the waiting room. He looked pale, weak, and annoyed. Now, looking back, he was probably more worried than anything.

My cousin waited in the common area while my family went back with the medical assistant. She began asking my dad identifying questions to make sure she had the correct patient. Then she started the preliminary exam of his vital signs. When she left, we all sat in silence, not knowing what to expect from this visit and hesitantly eager to know the real seriousness of his condition.

Not much later, the nurse practitioner came in to begin her exam and evaluation of my father. She asked multiple duplicate questions that the MA already asked, which irritated my father. My sister and I understood this process and appreciated that it functions to reduce the risk of mistaken patient identity and to create consistency with medical history for correct documentation. However, these processes and best practices did not matter to my dad. He only knew he had to repeat himself multiple times, and it required energy he didn't have.

My sister had been saying for the past few months that our dad was depressed and if we could get him past his misery, he would be fine. I was not around enough to agree or disagree. She was much more present since she lived closer to them. When the nurse practitioner asked my dad about feelings of depression, he sort of nodded with a sideways noncommittal answer of half yes and half no. She asked if there was any family history of depression. He said with a low voice, "yeah…my mother." Then she asked him if there was a history of suicidal ideation in the family.

He looked up at the ceiling, contemplative, and then said, "Yeah… my mother….I remember one time when I was a young kid, about 10 or 11…She…(he choked up)…she said she was going to kill herself…

she was going to drive the car into a lake and drown herself…(he fought back tears)…She took off out of the driveway….I got on my bike… (he was struggling to speak)…I rode as fast as my legs could pedal to catch her…I couldn't pedal fast enough…" He was holding back from breaking down, his face became sullen, his distant gaze now on the floor. His memory opened a wound as fresh as if it happened yesterday.

My sister and I inconspicuously eyed each other. We knew of this grandmother, but we never knew this story. The nurse paused her questions, giving my dad time to share more or gain his composure. He fell completely silent. She was compassionate and agreed that must have been extremely difficult, then following protocol she had to ask him, "Do you have suicidal thoughts?"

He was still staring down, lost in his thoughts with ancient memories. He did not answer and just sort of shook his head no. The rest of the exam focused more on his shortness of breath, physical decline, the location of his pain, and the timing of when and how it started. She finished, what I'm sure felt like an interrogation to my dad and left the room.

My dad was getting more tired even though he was still just sitting in the wheelchair. The very act of being in it made him weak. I was not sure if he was exhausted from whatever it was that he was suffering from or if his mental recollection of chasing his mother on his bike wore him out. It was emotionally disturbing for me to hear that story. Who knows how many times it happened? I was only two years old when that grandmother passed of a massive heart attack at the young age of 59.

Soon the pulmonologist entered, introduced himself to each of us, shook our hands then spoke directly to my father. He began asking the same questions that the medical assistant and nurse practitioner did, my dad shook his head in irritation, "I've already told them…" He was fatigued, irritated, and wanted to know why it felt like he was being stabbed by a butcher knife.

After a thorough exam and asking pointed questions, the physician suggested further testing. He ordered a full PET scan to confirm his suspicion of mesothelioma. My father was diagnosed more than 20 years ago with asbestosis and considering the constant build-up of fluid around his lungs, the location and severity of the pain, he was confident in his diagnosis but wanted confirmatory testing. He dictated the prescription for the test to the nurse, and we took the earliest appointment available. Sadly, it wasn't until the end of the following month.

The distant look on my father's face was hard to read and I was not about to pose any more questions. We all went to lunch afterward, thinking this ritual would provide some normalcy to a day that was anything but.

Food was my dad's love language. In fact, he thought about food all the time and would ask my mom "What's for lunch?" over breakfast and what was for dinner while consuming lunch. But he was not interested in eating lately and today didn't change that. His lack of appetite was our biggest clue that something was seriously awry.

25

"Whatever will be, will be..."

Doris Day
Entertainer Extraordinaire

My dad's recollection of chasing after his mother on his bike as she drove away played on repeat in my mind. The vision of him as a young boy pedaling as fast as his legs could, with his heart both racing and breaking at the same time, crushed me. Where did this sit in his memories as a child and throughout his life? He kept it hidden well.

What else didn't I know about my father's internal struggles? Would it be healing or harmful to ask him about it? Assuming I would have opportunities in the future to talk with him, I put it on the back burner.

At the beginning of the year, my daughter asked if we could plan a "girls' trip" to California that summer. I had never been on one, and loved the idea of visiting anywhere in California, spending time with her, and trekking on a fun adventure. She suggested it, she planned it, and I paid for it.

We had no idea at that time the roller coaster our lives would ride over the months leading up to our vacation on the sunny coast of California. Fortunately, with our plans in place we had something positive and fun to hold onto while navigating our turbulent health scares.

I felt my dad was physically stable after my recent visit accompanying him to the Cleveland Clinic. Despite his 20-pound weight loss in a few short months, I assumed he was good enough for us to go.

I visited with him and my mom the weekend before leaving. While enjoying our conversation about my upcoming trip we decided to look on the Rand McNally Road Atlas to find exactly where in California we were going. We had relatives who lived on the West Coast and wondered if we would be close enough to visit them. It was at that moment when I saw how close we were going to be to San Francisco. I suggested to my daughter that we add that to our trip itinerary and she agreed.

It was the first week of June when we landed mid-morning at the San Jose, California airport and went to pick up our convertible rental car. The agent told us the only one they had on the lot was a Chevy Camaro, which I thought sounded fast and very cool.

My daughter and I followed the car rental signs to the garage that housed the rental cars and what was before our eyes? My favorite color, a bright yellow Chevy Camaro! Our first sign that this trip was about to be something special.

Of course, a convertible must be driven with the top down in sunny California. We quickly settled our luggage in the trunk, pushed the button to recoil the top and let the open sky be our guide as we embarked on the journey to San Francisco. As we pulled away from the airport, we let vacation joy fill our senses with sunshine, blue skies, and high anticipation of the never-before-seen landscape of central California.

Speeding away from the parking lot, we transformed into two blonde "California Girls" driving on the freeway of life. About 20 minutes into the drive up the mountains, we were two frozen blondes on this California "freezeway." Who knew it would be 40 degrees in the Golden state in June? Not me. The sun was shining, but it was no match for the chill through the mountains. We had the heat cranked on the highest setting, the hoods on our sweatshirts covered our heads and faces as much as possible without obstructing our vision. By the time we arrived in San Francisco, my hands lost all color and feeling, and were frozen stiff to the steering wheel.

Our first and very brief stop was the Golden Gate Bridge, another misconception as it was not golden or any hue of yellow at all. It was red. We noticed Alcatraz in the distance and quickly got back in the car to get warm, then explore downtown San Francisco. After we thawed, we thoroughly enjoyed a wonderful brunch at a local corner diner overlooking a park in the center of the city. Our waiter looked like Hugh Jackman, a resemblance that we readily registered because we'd seen "The Greatest Showman" at least seven times earlier that year.

We then walked the streets of San Francisco, impressed with and in awe of the steep hills, slanted architecture, historic buildings, and various micro-sized businesses nestled in this huge city. We went into a bridal boutique, only because our favorite show was "Say Yes to the Dress." We passed pizza shops (my husband's and my dog Lucky's favorite food of choice for any meal) and a place called Betty Lou's, which resonated with me because it was the name of one of my special residents at the retirement village. We were only a few hours into our first mother/daughter girls' trip and everything we were experiencing kept signaling that we came to the right place at the right time.

After walking around the part of town with restaurants, churches, businesses, and residences, we drove around the city. The visibility in this car was not the best and traveling on these iconic streets was one of the most frightening drives of my life. Approaching the top of the street, we were not able to see the ground in front of the hood, making us feel like we were falling off the edge of the earth. The winding turns proved nearly impossible to navigate, so I barely drove faster than 10 miles per hour or as slow as those behind me would tolerate.

Driving up the hills, I only saw the sky and rooftops reminding me of the nerve wracking ascent on a roller coaster. I remembered watching television shows and movies with cars racing through these streets. Obviously, those scenes were produced with trick photography, and/or highly trained stunt drivers.

The remainder of our trip was spent in a rental house near Carmel and Monterey. To my great delight, I discovered an inn in Carmel once owned by one of my all-time favorite classic movie stars, Doris Day. We walked through the lobby full of movie memorabilia from her career and life as one of the hardworking Hollywood Glamour girls. I longed to own her wardrobe; her style was exquisite, and her clothes are as fashionable now as they were then.

She was also classy, quirky, and from Ohio, making us almost like kinfolk. I had no idea when I gave my daughter complete reign over our plans, they would include the community where she lived, owned a business, and saved animals.

There was a coffee table book at our rental house featuring Clint Eastwood, a Hollywood legend, and my huband's favorite actor, and once mayor of the neighboring town of Carmel. I was humbled by this little nod from God.

Everything was within walking distance: restaurants, shopping, coffee, the ocean, running trails. We biked along the coast, listened to sea lions bark and watched the crashing of the waves in the Pacific Ocean. Every day was exactly what a vacation should be: relaxing, outdoor activities, breathtaking nature, excellent dining, unique and local cafes, and quaint shopping.

The time with my daughter in an idyllic setting gave us the gift of unwinding and enjoying each other's company without any agenda and the much-needed stress release of the health woes our family was walking through.

Upon returning home, my first priority was to visit my parents. I called them once from California and talked briefly to both. It was a quick conversation, no different than any of our other ones, except my mom said my father was declining.

I couldn't believe my eyes when I arrived and saw him sitting in a wheelchair at the kitchen table, and my mom was feeding him. He wore a terrycloth bib around his neck to keep his clothes clean and could barely communicate. He'd lost ground quickly over the two weeks that had passed. I tried to hide my shock when I catalogued his paleness and extreme weak state.

I couldn't make sense of his rapid decline. My first concern was that he was overmedicated. I spoke to him while we were away, and he was talking fine. I questioned in my mind what was really going on.

Once the meal was over, I pulled my dad away from the table and asked if he wanted to go outside. His face lit up and with the help of those around us, we got the wheelchair out on the front porch. We sat together for a while, talking a bit. I shared details of our trip and even though he seemed a little distant, he was coherent.

When it was time to go back inside, I stood in front of him to help maneuver the wheelchair and he looked my way and said, "You get prettier every time I see you." I looked behind me to see who he was talking to. But there was no one else there. I immediately thought he was hallucinating; I recognized this from working in long-term care and seeing the effect of over medicated patients. Then I realized he was looking directly at and talking to me.

He had never uttered those words to me in my lifetime that I was pretty. Compliments were never a thing in our house. We did not exchange insults and we loved each other very much, but we did not offer compliments. That was when I knew my father was seriously ill. Something happens to individuals when they know and accept that they are at the end of their lives.

My heart melted at my father's kind and sincere words. It made me feel as pretty as he saw me to be and gave me the confidence to take charge. After a few hours without pain meds, he was much more coherent, and I thought strong enough to go for a car ride.

I convinced my mother and sister that we could take him to Dairy Queen, the same one that we frequented after our childhood softball games. We were able to get my dad in my mom's minivan and we drove to get hot fudge sundaes because ice cream always makes life better.

My dad smiled, talked and we were together, the four of us, my sister and I in the backseat just like when we were kids. I thought about the times we traveled and my parents' commitment to our family vacations every summer. Later on, they willingly and happily traversed the country to see their children and grandchildren.

Their spirt of adventure coupled with their devotion to the grandchildren took them to Las Vegas, the Carolinas, Florida, and various states in between. And now just a few blocks from our home, I was afraid this might be my dad's last joy ride in a car.

26

"Blessed is the man who trusts in the Lord, whose trust is the Lord. He is like a tree planted by water..."

Jeremiah 17:7 ESV

The following weeks, I returned to my parents' home on weekends to help with his care. I volunteered to take the night shift so my mom could get some rest. Every time in the middle of the night when my dad called out, I reassured him, "I'm right here, dad." Even though my heart broke watching his will and strength slowly fade, it was an honor to support him, my mom, and sister.

For the first time in over a year, I was grateful to be away from the retirement village. Not away from the people, but the constraints of the position that required me to be available 24/7 for the admission process. I was only alloted two weeks' vacation and spent that time over the holidays with my children. If I were still in that role, I would never have been present for my mom and dad during this crisis.

His rapid decline still did not make sense. The questions were plenty but answers few. I knew hospice was excellent at pain management and I encouraged that we get those services involved. My parent's family physician, along with the lung and heart doctors, had been suggesting hospice for months.

Dad had no fight in him, and mom was desperate to make him well again. Our call to hospice was, in my eyes, an attempt to manage his pain and not a surrender flag that his life was ending.

We did not have a confirmed diagnosis and hospice discouraged us from getting more tests asking, "What would it change?" He had asbestosis and we highly suspected he was suffering from worsening mesothelioma from his years working in the sheet metal industry and repairing cars and motorcycles. He quit smoking twenty years ago, although I think he snuck a couple here and there when he was anxious or upset about something.

He was not communicating much, eating even less and was unable to walk or even stand on his own. He needed care around the clock and while my mom did all she could to care for him, keep him comfortable and meet every need possible, my dad became too much for her to handle alone.

My sister helped through the week, and I spent weekend nights by my father's bedside as he restlessly tried to get comfortable. I wanted to fix whatever was ailing him just like he could fix anything in our house and on wheels.

I wasn't accepting his quick decline and deeply regretted not being more involved with his care and diagnosis to grasp the abrupt halt to his life. Or was it quick? I hadn't been around for the past several months to have a real understanding. Reflecting in this moment, I hadn't been attentive for many years.

Was it asking too much of me to call him more often, or follow him to the garage, or help move the porch furniture? As his health worsened, the more I kicked myself for not being available for him the way he was always present and available for me and my family.

On the last Saturday in June, he was exceptionally agitated through the night. We were up and down several times. It was around 5 a.m. and I could not fall back to sleep, so I decided to read my daily devotion at my father's bedside while holding his hand and he was finally able to rest.

My father was not a praying kind of guy. He may have prayed in silence and solitude somewhere/sometime, but I never knew it. He and my mom were highly active with a variety of events in the church and attended mass religiously every weekend, but again, I had no knowledge if they read the bible or prayed, or neither.

I moved closer to my dad. I sat in a folding chair next to his bed and read my devotion quietly out loud, not to him, but to include him in my morning conversation with God. I started with my favorite scripture, Jeremiah 17:7-8 NASV, "Blessed is the man who trusts in the Lord and whose trust is the Lord. For he will be like a tree planted by the water, that extends its roots by a stream and will not fear when the heat comes; but its leaves will be green, and it will not be anxious in a year of drought nor cease to yield fruit."

Closing my bible and devotional book, I held my father's hand and whispered some of the words from the song, No Matter What by Ryan Stevenson. I did not remember all the words, I sang bits and pieces, the gist of the song is that regardless of what we've been taught or things we've done in the past, we will always be God's children and He loves us.

I wanted him to know that no matter what happened in his life that God loved him, no matter what. I also told him that he was a good father, husband, uncle, son, friend, brother, grandfather, great-grandfather, neighbor, a hard-working ethical man, and talented sheet metal worker. I wanted him to hear from me that he was smart, kind, generous and a genuinely good man who always provided for his family, and we were blessed to have him. Words I never shared with him while he was well.

I sat by my father's side, trying to comprehend the heartache he wrestled with growing up with a mother who struggled with depression to the point of attempted suicide. Ever since he shared that memory at the doctor's office, I had a different view of my dad. I was sad for many reasons, but most of all that I never took the time to really know my dad and his personal history.

I knew he was the provider of our family, he worked hard at his job and just as hard at home around the house and would help anyone who needed it. I knew he loved to travel, attend church with my mom, socialize with friends and family, and enjoyed every motorcycle trip with his motorcycle buddies. Most of all, he was still crazy in love with my mom, even after fifty years of marriage, they had fun doing everything and anything together.

The previous year he shared with me his high school playbills from the plays that he was in. He knew my love of performing arts and thought I would want them. I never knew he was in the school plays.

I was too involved with my own family to take the time to develop a mature relationship with him. Regardless of my lack of knowledge about the details of his life, I wanted him to know that God loved him and saw everything he did for others and no matter what he had done or not done, God's love was unconditional.

A short while later, my mom woke up and came out of her room. I asked her if it was okay for me to go on a run. She said yes, but before I left, we changed my dad's sheets, got him cleaned up and changed his clothes. We were able to get him to sit on the side of the bed with his feet barely touching the floor, my mom was by his side supporting him.

I sat on the couch across from him and he asked with clear speech if my son was there. The one who bought his own motorcycle at the age of 21 and rode with my dad. I told him he was not, but he was coming into town later that afternoon.

He nodded his head in acknowledgement. His eyes had barely been open the past two weeks. They were opening and closing now with an empty gaze and agony filled his face. He coiled when anyone touched the right side of his rib cage. His right shoulder ached as well, stemming from an incident at the pain doctor more than a month ago.

He asked to stand, we stood on each side and helped him to his feet. It took all his strength to stand erect, lifting his head, attempting to stand independently. His bold stature lasted a few solid seconds then his weight pulled him back down to the bed. My mom and I helped position him comfortably in a reclining position, then I walked through the kitchen to leave for my run.

I had one foot out the door when I heard my mom say with alarm in her voice, "Hon, what is it?! What's wrong?!" Because of her tone, I turned back.

I saw my father's arms raised upward, reaching as if someone was offering to lift him. His eyes were opened wider than they had been in weeks and his mouth was opened as if he were saying something. I ran back to his side, I yelled for my sister who was asleep in the guest room. She quickly joined us at my father's bedside as he took a few brief breaths. His arms fell at his sides, eyes closed, no more breaths, his body no longer in pain, no more pain. He was gone. I knew he was gone, I prayed over him, "absent from the body present with the Lord. I love you, Dad."

27

*"The Lord is near to the brokenhearted and
saves those who are crushed in spirit."*

Psalm 34:18 NASV

My mother, sister, and I stood exceptionally still in the deafening
silence surrounding my father, staring in disbelief at his shell of a body
while a steady stream of tears saturated our exhausted faces. Hoping
that if we looked long enough, he would breathe again or open his eyes,
we knew it wouldn't happen. Nor could we fathom he was really gone -
so quickly, so immediately, so permanently.

My sister called the hospice nurse, my mother and I remained in
our caregiver position at his side. He was at peace; we were in shock. A
few weeks ago, we were getting ice cream sundaes. We prayed for his
pain to end, but not for him to leave this earth to make it happen. Our
minds unable to wrap around the speed of his decline.

The nurse arrived, completed a brief exam, and declared the time
and date of his death. My childhood home, my life, my heart, my mom,
my sister…never the same.

We called the funeral home and lingered in a daze around my father
as his body lie in the hospital bed in our family room. While waiting, we
started making the dreaded phone calls to family members and friends.
Almost immediately, my older cousin arrived knowing exactly how to
help us through this immediate period of aftershocks. Her parents were
deceased, my aunt and uncle (her dad and my dad were brothers and
best friends) and she knew how to navigate this time of intense grief

and decision-making.

When the funeral home workers arrived, much too soon, my mom instructed them to handle my father's body with the utmost care and respect. She explained how my grandmother was nearly dropped by funeral home personnel and she was not going to let that happen to her husband. My cousin encouraged us to leave the room while they placed my father in a body bag. She was right, no one should witness that of a loved one. But as soon as that part was done, my mother supervised to ensure they held on as tight as she would to my father as they took him from our home.

Every step they took toward the van in the driveway chipped away at my heart. My mom hovered to ensure they were gentle and moved cautiously from the living room to the van. The mental, physical, and emotional toll proved all-encompassing when watching a loved one take their last breath, be declared dead, and carried off in a body bag. The entire process pounded my entire body, leaving me beaten to a pulp.

By contrast, my mom, in a state of shock and nervous energy, kept moving and began activating funeral plans. Most of the details were already known, my parents believed in planning ahead. They wanted to make their own decisions about the casket and did it together. A few years prior they oddly enjoyed a visit to the funeral home to make their final decisions in advance. They joked about that being one of the most memorable shopping excursions of their lives.

With being active members in the church and personal friends with the funeral home director, those calls were done without hesitation. Other phone calls were placed, the florist picked, the plans confirmed, the obituary sent to the newspaper and the calling hours scheduled for the next day.

One of my first phone calls after calling my husband was to reach out to Lydia. I shared with her how I prayed beside my father in his last hour. I wanted her to know how her star pupil responded with faith on her darkest day. I shared how I felt the presence of God when my father passed, and the peace and knowledge I had of my dad's immediate entrance into heaven. All of this was made possible because of her bible study.

My gratitude ran deep for our time in her condo and our continued fellowship. It was because of her leadership and living example of a close relationship with God, and then sharing it with us, that allowed me to face this awful loss with a sense of calm.

When his obituary was published in the afternoon newspaper, the phone began ringing off the hook and people brought food or stopped by to offer support. The house took on an atmosphere of a social event; planning menus, estimating the number of mourners, displaying artifacts, choosing types and colors of flowers, music selections, contacting the choir director, confirming pall bearers, reviewing the scriptures chosen for Mass and deciding who will read and bring up the gifts.

Numerous details needed instant decisions when all I wanted to do was sit, cry, and think about my dad. But my mom was, and always will be a woman of action. When she is nervous or stressed, she must be doing something and this situation of losing her lifetime companion and best friend, launched her into hyper-active mode.

I woke up the next morning to an eerily quiet and emptier home. I began my morning prayer, devotion, and run routine with more intensity than usual. When I stood at the threshold of our backdoor, even though the door was open, something made me pause.

Just 24 hours ago when I stood in that same doorway poised to go outside, my father was on the doorstep of heaven. When I stepped out and back in, he stepped into the next realm. During that simultaneous moment, I fully believe with all my heart that he was reaching up to God or his father or mother or brother. Someone in heaven was extending his or her arms to my dad. I saw it in his eyes and by the look on his face, a look of joyful anticipation, he wanted to go with whoever was reaching for him.

I moved through the doorway's forcefield of heaviness to run on this sunny and perfectly cool summer morning. I ran down our street and made a left turn onto another street and the first thing I saw, made my heart skip a beat, a 1960-something sky blue Corvair turning the corner and going in the direction of the church. Illusion or not, I sprinted to see it, to catch it, because my father's spirit was in that car taking himself on yet another joy ride.

I felt an adrenaline rush to catch the car and immediately pictured him chasing after his mother's car while riding his bike. I pursued that car with every muscle in my body. I know my dad's body was not in the car, but to me my dad was every classic car and motorcycle. Thinking that my dad was permanently gone, and I would never get to see him on this earth again, pulled my heart out of my chest as the car left my sight.

As soon as I returned home, I penned his eulogy with every thought and memory that flooded my mind while running. Later, when the time came for calling hours, nothing could have prepared me to see my father in his casket. Even though my dad's body was still with us, his spirit was gone, making the hours spent in the presence of his body a time of deep sadness. I wanted to turn back the clock, hug him and not let go, and apologize profusely for not being kind enough to him, or available enough, or interested enough in what mattered to him.

The funeral home staff did their trained best to make my father look natural, but he wasn't one to wear heavy cake makeup. Surely, the funeral home industry could update their products, after all this was not a 1920s silent movie.

My mother insisted our immediate family wear name tags so that people knew the family members. No one had the heart to deny her this request. Every decision for the past month, and especially now, was hers to make. We were not going to disagree with a woman who had just lost her best friend and the love of her life for more than 57 years over something as insignificant as wearing name tags. It was not enough to put our names on the sticker, we had to list our relationship to my father. We said, "Sure, Mom. Anything you want."

After being introduced to and greeting more than 150 people from every segment of my parents' lives, I understood the purpose of the name tags and appreciated not having to introduce myself, my husband, and our four children by name and relation to every person who passed through on an exceedingly difficult late Sunday afternoon. The line of mourners started at four o'clock and did not stop until eight o'clock. I never expected the multitudes of people from every stage of my father's life. There were childhood friends, high school classmates, cousins, old neighbors, new neighbors, people from the church, union brothers, even an old boss. My sister and I shouted the boss' name when he re-introduced himself to us as we stood next to my father's casket, "DON KECK!" He was at least six inches shorter than when we last saw him 45 years ago.

The stream of people never slowed. We wept with his motorcycle buddies, my parent's friends, my mother's exercise groups, former colleagues, my in-laws and friends, my sister's in-laws, and friends. The weight of sorrow was shared by multitudes of caring supportive people. And all I heard throughout the night were fond memories: "I loved your dad"…"He was my favorite"…"Your dad always took care of my car and never charged me"…"Your dad was always there for me"…"Your dad was voted funniest in our class"…"Your dad was one of the best friends I ever had"…"Your dad could diagnose my car problem over the phone"…"Your dad gave us gas money"…."Your dad took care of…"…"Your dad made sure…" …Your dad…" One great comment and memory after another … all night long. I never knew how much he meant to others and what he did for so many people.

The night was as draining as it was comforting, standing there beside my father, greeting everyone, crying with them, listening to their stories, reminiscing. Prior to this, I never really understood the purpose of calling hours. I thought it was morbid and grueling for the family to stand beside their deceased loved one and talk to people for hours. But then I was never "that" person, I only attended calling hours as one of the mourners going through the line, not the one by the casket.

After being on the recipient end of those offering condolences, I fully understood and had a new appreciation for the comfort and peace that comes from the presence of family and friends during tremendous heartbreak. Their friendship and support gave me the strength to make it through. Without experiencing this tradition, I never would have known the impact my father had in the lives of so many others and how much it meant to me hearing all the wonderful things my father did for them. I rewrote my father's eulogy that night based on the experience from calling hours.

28

"I just want one more look at you."

A Star Is Born (all four versions)

The next day at the funeral was much of the same. The church was full of caring, grieving people sharing their presence to support us. As I stood at the altar giving my father's eulogy, the weight of my sorrow lifted a little as I looked into the sea of mutually sad faces. My heart was not as heavy when it was being held by numerous family members, friends, and people I never knew.

I asked the crowd, "Please take a moment to think about something my father did for you, because I know everyone in this church was the recipient of something kind and selfless from my father." I gave them time to think, and the communal feeling of great loss palpated through the pews. I finished the eulogy with tears in my eyes and a gaping hole in my heart.

My son drove my father's motorcycle behind the hearse in the procession from the church to the cemetery. I know that must have been one of the hardest things he ever did. He only got one chance to ride beside my father before my dad had to give up riding.

My mom wanted to see my father all the way to the end. We gathered around his grave for the final blessing and watched his casket as it lowered into the ground. We threw a handful of dirt and some flowers into the grave, then stood back to watch the grounds crew meticulously top the casket with the rest of the dirt.

When it was time to leave, something came over me and I decided to ride with my son on my father's motorcycle even though I was still in my suit and heels. I believed it was an opportunity that I would never have again. The Holy Spirit whispered for me to do something extraordinary at that moment. It was wild, free, and I felt my father riding with us.

The month leading up to my father's passing was mentally and physically exhausting as we navigated the high hopes of his health improving and the deep disappointment of reality. The passing of my father was unexpected and not without enormous regret. Regret over not asking enough questions about his health and the cause of his intense pain, regret over not pushing for more tests for a definitive diagnosis, regret for not looking into possible treatments or clinical trials to treat mesothelioma, regret over not being able to fix my father's health the way he fixed anything anyone asked of him.

The biggest regret was not spending enough time with my dad as a grown adult daughter. All he ever wanted was to teach me, love me, provide for me, laugh with me, and enjoy my family. And all I ever gave him were excuses about being too busy. I will never get another chance to make up for lost time or show him how much I loved him in return.

There was a little space in my heart that was grateful for being present and available for him, my mom, and my sister when they needed me the most that final month. I will never forget his weakened voice calling out in the night for help as he lay in the hospice bed next to the couch where I slept as best as I could. I remembered that I was quick to respond and moved to his bedside reassuring him of my presence. And I recalled the relief on his face as he settled down, able to rest again. Those memories were a balm on my wounded spirit.

On the evening of the funeral, my mom and sister and our families sat around the kitchen table at my parents' house reminiscing through tears and laughter, holding onto every memory. My father would have been in his element among our family circle telling stories. My son looked out the front window and told us to look, be still our hearts when we saw a 1957 Chevy cruising down the street. It was a bittersweet moment because that was the one car my dad would always spot, announcing, "That's a '57 Chevy." We knew it was my father's way of saying hello from heaven. While it was an exhausting day, we encircled my mom with our love and presence, certain it was going to be difficult for her to retire into an empty bed.

I didn't pinpoint the exact day when I would return home to Cincinnati. I woke up the next morning open to and available for whatever my mom needed, "playing it by ear" as my parents used to say. After a quiet morning without much conversation, our minds occupied with the enormity of my father's absence, we were unable to navigate the new normal. We didn't know how to exist with this obvious and immeasurable void missing from our hearts and home.

By early afternoon when all the busyness of the last few days came to a halt, my mom said she would be okay and told me to go home to my family. I asked her if she was sure, and in her words, she said "I have to be."

It was the loneliest and longest car ride, my eyes never dried. It was impossible to grasp the course my father's life took this past month. That evening as I unpacked my thoughts and suitcase alone in my bedroom, I needed a break from the suffering and shock of it all. If only for a moment, not to forget my father or to move on, but a gentle distraction from the white rapids of emotions drowning my heart and mind.

The finality of never hearing my father's voice again or seeing his smile or that he would never, ever, be there when I needed him, was too much to process. All I wanted was to shut out the world, and not face reality.

This was the moment TCM swooped in and cradled me with the loving arms of my beloved father. I turned on the television without regard for the scheduled movie, it was after the introduction and background story and several minutes into the movie. Seeing it from the beginning didn't matter, because at this juncture it wasn't about the movie, it was about numbing the pain.

As I described in the first chapter, the movie caught my attention immediately with the late 1960s fashion, hairdos, cars, and location. It was the perfect distraction from my current state of heartbreak. When that handsome man in the doorway, Steve McQueen, looked through the television directly into my tear-filled eyes with his piercing blue eyes, I was never the same again. What followed was a cavalcade of connections to my father that blew my mind and filled my soul.

The parallels between Steve and my father's personal lives; motorcycles, classic cars, Irish heritage, and deaths related to mesothelioma, and his character in this specific movie became the most extraordinary mystical loving experience of my life. Of all McQueen's movies, it had to be this exact one, at this exact time, with a classic car and genuine lead character. There wouldn't have been a connection if it were one of Steve's military themed movies, or when he played a con man, bank robber, gambler, or prisoner. None of those would have meant anything to me and my father.

This movie continued to connect with me via a VW Beetle, fingerprints to solve the murder, the setting in San Francisco where I had just visited weeks prior, and the peeling of the car tires. All of it opened the hole in my heart wider, and I deeply missed my father and his voice. Then, almost simultaneously, I was overcome with a peaceful presence making it clear that my father was still with me and would always be with me.

Turning to TCM for pain relief opened the door to the holy universe who connected Steve McQueen and the movie Bullitt with my father and tied them to my soul. I didn't ask for a sign, it was a moment of complete brokenness and surrender of the pain, regret, and shock of his death. The almighty love of God knew exactly what I needed and how to deliver a message from heaven that my father and God are with me, always, everywhere, and forever.

Thinking about it, my father's first real job was working at a Ford dealership, Welch Motors. As a child, I remember visiting the showroom whenever my dad got the inkling to check out the newest models, and to catch up with the people he knew since his childhood. My parents only purchased one new car in my childhood, and it was a Ford Thunderbird. The first car my parents purchased for me when I got my driver's license was a yellow Ford Maverick. Which makes it even more personal that God would use a Ford vehicle to deliver a message from heaven.

Naturally, my dad would come to me from the afterlife via a car, not just any car, the most famous movie car in classic movie history, the green mustang also a Ford product. I could always count on my dad to come to my rescue when I had a car crisis. Whether it was a flat tire, or bad spark plug, or a dead battery, my dad would drop whatever he was doing to be at my side and get me on my way.

I will never forget the time I drove three hours to see my boyfriend at college and my car died just as I exited the freeway. Back then we didn't have cell phones, and I used a pay phone to call my dad who immediately called his brother, my Uncle Dale, and together they drove the 300-miles-round trip to save the day. He never lectured me on what I should have done differently, nor arrived aggravated at being inconvenienced. He cared too much about me and my safety on the road to be angry. He was an automobile expert and will always be synonymous with cars in my mind and fondest memories.

This surreal movie miracle was my "road to Damascus flash of enlightenment" like Saul of Tarsus. Except it was a street in San Francisco with superstar Steve McQueen. Just like Saul, I was not worthy of a holy moment. My brain wouldn't let go of all the things I should have said and done with my father, and all the things I should not have said and done. I never expected our time together to end so abruptly and the pain was made worse with such distance to our relationship. I loved my father dearly, but never told him often enough or shared how much he meant to me.

Those opportunities are gone from this earth as much as he is. From this pit of darkness, God came to me where I was and in a way only a divine being could know the unique connection between my father and me. The timing of my job change allowed me to be with him in the end, the timing of my trip to San Francisco, the timing of Bullitt with Steve McQueen and Lt. Frank Bullitt was as much of a holy experience as anyone in the bible and those children who saw Mary in the clouds.

I heard God's whisper and all of heaven showering me with peace and comfort, "Your dad is with you, and he will always be with you. And so am I." It was electrifying and calming, odd yet ordinary, and uniquely specific to me, a true blessing in my bedroom. The very place where I begin and end every day. The private space where I rest, dream, worry, pray, read, cry, and take refuge from the world. This could never have happened if I kept God in a box in a church.

I truly believe God is beyond our finite minds, it's like trying to contain the ocean in a mason jar. I found Catholicism teaches narrow minded thinking, exclusivity, and is a financial and man-centered culture.

Thankfully, and fascinatingly, The Creator of the universe can't be, won't be confined, defined, or maligned by man. I am eternally grateful to have been privy to sermons and worship music via the radio, attended various churches, spent time in God's word and with Lydia, and read authors who helped open my heart and eyes to God's truth. If I hadn't been exposed to being outside the Catholic church, I would have missed one of the greatest blessings of my life.

The whole experience crossed a threshold for my dad and I to have a new and transformed relationship. He was gone from this earth, but our connection was stronger than ever. No more distance between us, only love and respect. I was humbled and thrilled to be gifted with the knowledge that those who pass away never really leave us.

29

"Sometimes you have to say goodbye to the things you know and hello to the things you don't."

Steve McQueen
Actor

Four months later, watching TCM as usual, one of the hosts asked, "Do you have a special connection to a movie? A story that shares your love of classic movies?" I responded to the television, "Yes, I do!" Recalling the night Bullitt and my father enveloped my heart and soul. They were searching for 25 viewers to dedicate and introduce a movie with the main host. All we had to do was submit a brief video telling our story about our connection to the movie.

That invitation set my imagination into high gear. I had the perfect story. Months of meditating on the whole mystical experience, I recalled the scripture about a man who died and asked the Divine to communicate with his family about the afterlife. God denied that request, but I believe the universe honored my father's request to tell me that he was still with me and, there was most assuredly an afterlife. Unlike when he was on this earth and I wouldn't listen, he knew how to speak to me in a way that I would hear and understand. He asked God to ease my pain and the spiritual universe responded by assigning the coolest angel in heaven, Steve McQueen, to collaborate with my father and surround me with their presence and profound love.

Immediately after learning the details of the contest submission, my head spun like a Tilt-A-Whirl giving ride to every idea that came to mind. The first plan I ran with was to film from my yellow VW Beetle and peel the tires as I drove away replicating the iconic chase. I asked my husband how one peels the tires of a car. After he questioned my question, and without sharing the why behind my question, he explained that I cannot peel the tires on my bug because it was a front wheel drive. Again, he asked me why I would want to do such a thing, but it wasn't necessary to elaborate, so onto Plan B.

Whatever I did, my attire had to match Frank Bullitt's outfit and style from the late '60s era. I chose a dark turtleneck, tan trench coat and mini skirt, and knee-high boots. I told the story to my camera phone standing by my yellow VW Beetle in our garage. It was okay, but I knew I could do better.

Plan C, the best one yet popped into my head - tape it in my dad's garage, surrounded by his tools, beside his motorcycle, in my father's happy place. YES!

With the contest rules of keeping the video to 90 seconds, I utilized cue cards. It was important to organize my thoughts, keep it brief, focus on the movie, speak clearly, and leave out the spiritual aspect. Tough task. Brevity is not my forte and the whole experience only happened because of divine intervention. But I knew better than to mix holiness with Hollywood.

I had not told my mom or anyone else in the family about my experience that night in my bedroom with Steve McQueen and my dad. It was personal and moreover, no one would understand the magnitude of the occurrence. I asked for my daughter's artistic feedback and assistance in making the video. She thought it was cool, believed my story, and encouraged me to record it out of town in my parents' garage.

The following weekend when our family was in Youngstown it was a chilling 30 some degrees outside and so was the garage. I needed their help, so I explained the contest and the experience behind my movie dedication. Without question, they were on board to help regardless of the cold temperature.

Once in the garage, we pushed my dad's motorcycle out of the storage side and into the main area by his tools and workshop area. My son pointed to something on my father's motorcycle, and when I saw it, I froze and melted at the same time. My dad's motorcycle was a Royal

Enfield "Bullet!" Chills raced through my body. I did not know this fact the night the movie came into my world. My dad's final model of motorcycle echoed his message from beyond that he was fully present that night and always.

It's also safe to assume it was a motorcycle that my father's outstretched arms and hands reached for upon his last breath. Perhaps Steve met him at the gates of heaven with a Triumph motorcycle as they rode to meet St. Pete.

My mom, sister, and future daughter-in-law held cue cards. My husband and son both recorded on their phones as I told my story. I cried, my mom cried, my sister cried, and I messed up my words and started to ramble. After 30+ more attempts and not getting it to my perfection, our time nearly expired as we had another commitment. We took a break and accepted that we would try again later. After a few hours to regroup and rehearse, I nailed the video within the allotted time.

I submitted it to TCM on November 11th hoping that specific day would bring me good luck because my daughter was born at 11:11 a.m. and it was Veteran's Day. My grandfather and my husband's grandfather proudly served in WWII, many of my residents from the retirement village were veterans, as was Steve McQueen.

I hoped that my video would be chosen for the 25th year celebration. I accepted the odds were against me, as I assumed to be competing against thousands of people across the country who had equally great stories.

As much as I wanted to win, after my finger hit the submit button, the result was released to the jury at TCM headquarters and to the power of movie-loving angels in heaven. It would be a real kick if I were selected, yet the ultimate honor was when heaven and earth joined forces in my bedroom through an old movie for a powerful, unforgettable spiritual experience.

30

"Three things cannot be long hidden: the sun, the moon, and the truth."

Buddha

It was the first week of December when I was in Miami, Florida for the last sales meeting of the year. I hadn't been to Miami since my field trip to a fashion school with our Wendy Ward Teen Board in the early 1980s. I was thrilled to be going anywhere above freezing, and being oceanside was butter on warm bread. The location gave me something to look forward to.

Typically, I dread meetings worse than housework, especially when they include role-playing and being confined to a conference room chair for eight hours while senior level management highlights territory sales metrics and data. Sales updates are fine when one's geography is knocking it out of the park, but when the goals are unattainable or unmet, that salesperson suffers public humiliation.

Preparation and participation for such meetings was as nerve-wracking and anxiety filled as teaching a teenager to drive. Practicing and then delivering the exact sales call verbiage with intelligence and business acumen was as unnatural to me as pitching a tent. Even more difficult, was maintaining company enthusiasm over multiple days, hobnobbing with colleagues and leadership, and the constant pressure to pass product exams pushed me to a breaking point.

To have this meeting at a hotel on the beach balanced my nervous energy. For the first time ever in my twenty-plus year career, I arrived a few days early along with my husband to enjoy sunny Florida. The hotel was a small boutique style and gave me a positive vibe for the meeting since it was the name of a luxury car. Not just any car, but one of my father-in-law's and maternal grandparent's favorite cars, a Cadillac.

The Cadillac Hotel was beachfront, and the weather a perfect eighty degrees and sunshine. With a combination like that, I had a premonition this wasn't going to be the worst work week ever.

It was somewhat relaxing since I was well prepared, my territory was performing well, and my boss was a wonderful human being. Plus, I enjoyed working for this small biotech company where the management and colleagues were good people. This was uncharacteristic of me to be calm and minimally stressed the week of a meeting. I attributed it to the ocean and the perspective life handed me this year with the unimaginable loss of my father, some former residents, and three friends.

With a few days to spare, my husband and I explored the town. South Beach was full of energy, ethnicity, fascinating history, and scantily clad people everywhere; it was an adventure of its own. One of the first sites we saw was a car rental lot with classic cars, a Packard was closest to the street. We nib nosed around the lot awing over the works of auto history, we sent pictures of us in front of the Packard to my father-in-law.

While walking along Ocean Drive with the ocean on one side and cafés and boutiques on the other, we stumbled upon an art store. I have a deep appreciation for the arts – painters, sculptors, photographers, performers, etc. for I do not have the talent to do any of it. It's mind boggling to understand where those ideas originate and how they create something out of their imagination.

One artist's work caught my attention, each piece was vibrantly full of bold colors and playfulness, and the store clerk encouraged us to visit the artist's studio down the street. We did, and along with his artwork was a temporary exhibition of the creation of a sand mandala. We never heard of a sand mandala before. We discovered it was a Tibetan Buddhist practice of creating a detailed piece of art, taking days to complete. The monks use a small straw to blow the tiniest of colored sand into a specific pattern. They stood bent over inches away from the work of art coming to life on the table in the middle of the gallery.

As awe-inspiring as the piece was, I was equally astonished after I inquired about what they do with the piece once completed. They wipe it away. Taken aback, I considered it a waste of time to create something so beautiful only to destroy it after days of delicate and back breaking work. We walked about the showroom, admiring the talent of the genius Brazilian artist, Romero Britto.

There were multiple pieces I would have loved to own. One in particular kept pulling me in, titled The Hug. It was a colorful painting of a small human caricature with outstretched arms, smiling exuberantly, measuring at least six feet wide and three feet tall.

It spoke to me, for I am a hugger, a strong, deliberate, spine crunching hugger. Wrapping my arms around someone exchanges positive energy, and when done correctly offers compassion and reduces stress and fear. Most important, hugs are proven to heal the soul. The piece was large enough to feel as if the whole divine universe was sending me a hug and encouraging me to keep squeezing the breath out of others. It captivated me. The price stymied me. We moved along to less expensive pieces and just window-shopped.

My husband left the following day, I submerged myself into the meeting, but The Hug and the sand art shared a parking space in my brain. I learned the closing ceremony for the Tibetan sand mandala was to be midweek, my meeting schedule was tight, and most likely I would not be able to attend. The more I contemplated it, the more educated I became about the wisdom of the Buddhist belief in the transitory nature of life.

Spending my sacred few moments of free time on the beach watching the waves come and go, I thought about the year as it had transpired. It began with losing one of my closest residents from the retirement village, then working through multiple medical diagnoses with friends and family, the loss of my father, the death of three girlfriends all younger than I, and facing my own mortality halfway through this life.

Contemplating my first positive business meeting happening in a warm and vibrant location during a year of great loss deepened my faith in a real spiritual presence. Experiencing the unique and colorful artwork taking days to create only to be wiped away, gave me pause to appreciate the full and beautiful lives created and now gone. I felt a hint of acceptance of their deaths and a heightened awareness of the sanctity and brevity of our lives on this earth.

My heart softened in the sacredness of the moment, filling my soul with peace, gratitude, and encouragement to be fully present. Only the undefinable undeniable holy universe could coordinate a much-needed mystical connection between this Irish Catholic girl, Tibetan Monks, and a Brazilian artist.

After reviewing the agenda for the meeting, I noticed an uncommon afternoon break of free time. That never happens in a pharma meeting, our schedules always start with breakfast meetings at 7:00 a.m. followed by intense all-day meetings until 5:30 p.m., with working lunches and team dinners to impress management. Allotted time in the afternoon for personal exploration was a miracle in and of itself. I cross-checked the art studio schedule for the closing ceremony of the mandala and after picking myself up off the floor, it was the exact timing of my free afternoon. I was going. When heaven opens a door that wide, one must walk faithfully over that blessed threshold.

The following day my manager met with me privately during lunch to let me know I was getting a raise and the amount of my bonus for the quarter. Both were significant and a miracle on top of a miracle. And just enough to consider purchasing The Hug without tapping into my IRA.

I raced to the studio so as not to miss any detail of the elimination process. The place was as full as my heart was for this gift of divine intervention yet again. We were told people would receive some of the sand in the mandala if they wanted. I wanted.

The ceremony began with the monks chanting in unison with deep voices and varying sounds, barely human, instruments joined in, including a drum, cymbals, and long brass horns. The combination of sounds mimicked the low decibel of a beating heart connecting with an energy pulsating through my body. A bell rang, and prayers were offered. I stood front and center to the meticulous wiping away of every grain of sand as it was done with gentle and purposeful intention. The sweeping away was as melodic as the music, and as artistic as the process to create it. Within my view, beyond the monks and their art, stood

Romero Britto and above him The Hug.

The symbolism of the impermanence of all that exists was not lost on me. During the ceremony, I held in my heart my father and friends who passed that year. All of whom were wonderful human beings with families, some young children, some with grandchildren and great grandchildren who would have enjoyed the wisdom of an elder. They were heartbreaking losses, beautiful lives, many layered lives of work, hobbies, and family woven into a full tapestry of experiences wiped out by disease. This was heavy for my heart yet healing for my soul. God cared enough about me to give me this moment in time as an ointment to my pain.

The mandala includes millions of grains of sand laid into place over a period of days or weeks to form a specific image. All mandalas have an outer, inner, and secret meaning. The outer level represents the world in its divine form, the inner level represents a map where the human mind is transformed into an enlightened mind, and the secret level represents the balance of the energies of the body and the light dimension of the mind. The creation is said to effect purification and healing in each of these levels. I testify to this process and its mystical and profound impact. The whole process is about letting go. I felt myself releasing the clutches of my sorrow and angst over losing my father and friends.

I was a firsthand witness to the creation and the goodbye of something worthwhile and beautiful. It wasn't unfair, or horrific, or a waste of time, it was life.

One of the monks kept his eye on me, sensing my connection to the sacred sand, and he gave me the first grains offered to the crowd. It was an honor to be present for this ceremony, a true and timely gift from above. Afterward I spoke with one of the studio experts and purchased The Hug. It hangs above my bed reminding me of God's loving arms around me and the precious and constant blessing of divine timing, peace, and impermanence of this life.

31

*"All the world's a stage and most of us
are desperately unrehearsed."*

Irish Proverb

Leaving the warmth of Miami for blustery Ohio is never a pleasant transition and exiting the plane into the brutally cold tunnel was like walking into an arctic vortex. Re-acclimating to bone chilling temperatures typically sucks the life out of me, but not on this dark winter's night, I was still awestruck from a positive experience at a sales meeting and sacred encounter at the art studio.

To catch up with reality, I listened to voicemail. It was around 10 p.m. and one message from an unknown number said, "Hello, this is Susana with Turner Classic Movies. We want to reach out and let you know we loved your video about your dad and your story with the movie 'Bullitt.' We want you to be one of our 25 fans to come to the studio and be a guest programmer. Please call me back as soon as possible to let me know if you still want to do it."

I froze, then screamed loud enough to vibrate the fiberglass walls, and nearly dropped my phone. Some guy asked me if I just won the lottery! I told him, "BETTER!" He looked at me sideways as what could be better than that.

I called her back immediately because I assumed she was calling me from Hollywood where it was only 7:00 p.m. her time and she said it was okay to call her back. She answered, a little groggy and rightfully annoyed, I told her who I was, her response, "It's really late." I apologized profusely and said, "I thought you were in California. I will call back tomorrow." She said, no it was okay and explained the whole process of how I will have a producer, a stylist, and a hair and makeup specialist. They will fly me in on Wednesday evening, tape the dedication on Thursday, have dinner with all the winners and executives with Turner Broadcasting that evening, and then fly home on Friday. She asked, "Do you think you could make that?" Without any hesitation, I confirmed, with an "absolutely!"

My own stylist, producer, on TCM…pinch me to make sure I am not dreaming. I was beyond elated, the adrenaline surged through my veins, and then she said, "But you can't tell anyone." She explained they had to confirm with all the winners, and after my producer contacted me, then I could share it with others. Hmmm. Sure.

We hung up, and I immediately texted my mom, sister, husband, and children. And told them they could not tell anyone. Then, I had to share it with my boss to approve time off, and swore him to secrecy. Once TCM and I confirmed all the travel plans and my producer contacted me, I was free to spread the word.

As I thought about my dedication and the details of what happened, I wondered if this could be the place to share my "testimony" that evangelicals expect of all Christians. Would the studio staff, executives and audience welcome my God moment story? I was torn about sharing the spiritual aspect or remaining secular on the serendipitous timing of the classic movie and my father. I didn't want eye rolling from the host or censored for offensive God language or labeled a Jesus freak. Moreover, I wanted them to offer me a job as a regular host with my own programming, knowing full well it's never a good idea to talk religion in an interview.

Thankfully, I had a month to think it over. I practiced over and over to keep my story concise with balancing the movie with the mystical.

My confirmation letter came and said "The limo" would pick me up and drive me to the airport. I anticipated an extraordinary experience, and it did not disappoint. The week I was scheduled to leave for Atlanta where the TCM studios are located, I took my company car to a Ford dealer because the "check engine" light was on.

While they were working on it, I found my way to the showroom to check out the newest models of vehicles and trucks. My eyes nearly fell out of my head when I saw the sleek sporty green 2019 brand new Ford Mustang Bullitt. It was a work of art in the exact green as the one in the 1968 movie. This 50th anniversary edition was tricked out with extraordinary speed and performance features honoring the original Mustang from the movie.

I was speechless as I looked this gift horse right in the mouth with yet another layer of connection to the movie. I sat in it, took pictures in the driver's seat, and stood in front of it like a model. I did my best to negotiate with the salesman on the price, explaining how special the car was and where I was going that week and why. While I could not get the price low enough to meet my budget, the car's presence in the showroom added another surreal moment with my father and my new favorite classic movie. God's choice of cars and direct messaging was as cool as Steve McQueen.

Wednesday morning came, the limo driver picked me up in the early morning hours, secured my bags in the trunk, opened my door and encouraged me to relax in the back seat. I felt like a movie star before leaving my driveway. After landing in Atlanta, I spotted my next limo driver holding the sign with my name, I waved both arms above my head, flashed a huge smile and shouted, "That's ME!" Queen of cool I am not.

The driver picked up another fellow TCM 25 Winner, and just like me was a huge fan of Ginger Rogers. We shared a limo, and he shared his story, it was a lovely start to a beautiful friendship. We had breakfast, in a quaint cafe with Tiffany style lamps and décor. We talked for hours about our favorite classic movie stars. He presented his collection of pictures, autographs, and his experience in the "biz" as a standup comedian with the likes of Jackie Mason.

I took the afternoon to wander around Atlanta, visiting the Margaret Mitchell house and seeing the very desk and room where she wrote "Gone with The Wind." I practiced my story over and over to keep it concise. TCM was only giving guest programmers 20 minutes with the host, and I did not want to leave out any details or talk inaudibly fast, and I decided to leave my spiritual experience for another show.

The next morning, I arrived in the lobby early enough to check out the gift shop. And the gift I got was another nod from God when I saw the artwork from the Brazilian artist I had just discovered in Miami a month ago. The shelf was full of his various sculptures and words – love, laugh, dream, happy – they all spoke to me.

It was obvious who the other novice guest host winners were in the lobby by the anxious, excited, and lost look on our faces. We were transported by a plain white passenger van to an unmarked building where Susan greeted us with her warm, welcoming, beautiful Hollywood smile. She looked like a movie star herself with long dark perfectly coiffed hair and her faux fur coat. TCM taped our segments in different shifts over two days, there were only four of us on this bus, the rest were coming throughout the day.

Everyone I met, including fellow winners, Turner staff members, my producer, director, assistant producer, assistant director, door guard, errand runner, sound people, lighting, camera, stylist, each had their specific task and were all as nice as Midwest town folk. I was hyper nervous, but they put me at ease with their detailed organization, hospitality, and professionalism. Each person I introduced myself to or vice versa told me how much he/she enjoyed my story and related a story about losing his/her own parent.

While I was thrilled to be a guest host on my favorite television channel, I was only having this thrill because of the special connection to a movie through my deceased father. I would give up this once-in-a-lifetime experience in a New York Minute to have my dad back.

There I was… on the set, in the TCM studio, under the lights, cameras aimed at me, all while sitting in the chairs and background that I viewed every day from my home television. I chose a very specific blue turtleneck sweater dress to honor Steve McQueen who made the blue turtleneck a fashion trend, and around my neck was the necklace with my dad's thumbprint. While TCM staff taped my conversation, I choked up with a few tears in my eyes, but did not ruin my make up.

I shared about hearing a chorus of angels in heaven sing and shout, "Your dad is with you and will always be with you!" But that was as spiritual as my comfort zone allowed, and after seeing the program air, those words lay on the editing floor.

Being on the set taping my segment was my new happy place, and I secretly prayed they would offer me a hosting job. I graciously offered to be a fill in when the regular hosts went on vacation, or host my own genre, or guest program on multiple occasions to introduce movies with stars from Ohio (as there are plenty.)

When all 25 winners went to dinner that night, the conversations echoed through the restaurant with energy and laughter elicited by a shared knowledge base. I met people from New York, Philadelphia, Texas and places in between. We may or may not have had anything in common, so we went with what we knew, classic movies, and it ignited an exchange of commonality and unity that electrified our discussion.

We did not talk about our jobs, families, marital status, children, or backgrounds. Our topics focused on nothing but old movies, movie stars and our favorite memories around them. The honor to be chosen as one of the winners underscored how the Divine continued to bless my experience with my father and Bullitt.

My spiritual experience of providential timing and clear loving message from Heaven was validated by the TCM family of caring individuals. God was clearly and fully present in the oddest and yet ordinary way. But I never said those words to the host, staff, or fellow winners. Gifted with a worldwide audience and meeting people from all over the country, I kept spiritual language out of all conversations, except the part about hearing angels sing. I was given an incredible evangelistic opportunity, and I choked.

Yet the serendipitous events continued. The actual Ford Mustang used in the movie was on display in the National Automobile Museum at the very time of my taping on TCM. Later that year a book and documentary would be released sharing the unknown story of Steve McQueen's spiritual journey.

The following year, on the exact anniversary date of the TCM taping, I happened to be home for lunch, and tuned into the Mecum live auto auction just as that very Ford Mustang from the movie and found in a barn in Tennessee was on the auction block. They needed crowd control as it was the largest live audience ever to witness one of the most famous cars go up for bid. The event set records as the most famous Mustang of all time and garnered a record breaking $3.74

million dollars. The engine was still powerfully purring as it rolled onto center stage just as it did throughout the 1968 movie.

The brief moment that started as fleeting and fragile as a snowflake with an offhand comment about needing a break from grieving my father's death compounded into an avalanche experience.

32

"Life is about timing."

Carl Lewis
Track and Field Olympian

One early morning, after my average routine of prayer and meditation, I left home in my gray Ford Escape to make sales calls in Indiana. Traveling east on Interstate 74 in southeast Indiana spreads flat, with boring terrain and minimal bends in the road. The drive can be mind-numbing monotonous just focusing straight ahead with nary an occasional 45-degree angle. The view included corn fields, a few horses, and some random manufacturing plants, but nothing too noteworthy to keep my attention. I kept myself entertained listening to the movie soundtracks from "The Greatest Showman" and "Momma Mia."

I continued to struggle with my father's death and cried almost every day. He was never out of my mind. He loved to travel by car and was a hard worker so when I was working and driving in my car, I always felt him with me just by thinking about him. I did not comprehend how much he was really with me on this seemingly ordinary commute until a wrapped car sped past and grabbed my full attention.

What I mean by wrapped was that it had logos all over it. It is common for businesses to advertise their logo, phone number, and slogan on cars and trucks, but this car was fully covered in lettering and colors so much so that I could not figure out what the business was or what kind of car it was. Then another one passed, just as colorful and this time I could tell it was a Porsche and I thought "now, that's a great company car." Then another one followed and it was a high-performance car. I looked in my rear-view mirror and along came more.

"*What* on earth was happening?!" I tried to read the cars as they flew by, but that proved impossible due to the extensive advertising messages. No car sported simple lettering that read "Harry's Electric" or a company name, and each passing ride grew in sticker price.

There was a slight lull, then more and more approached, and they were driving slightly over the speed limit, but finally I was able to see one of the cars and it said, "Gold Rush Rally." I had no idea what it was, but one thing was certain, I was in a real-life "Cannonball Run" hypercar convoy hauling a**! I sat straight up in my seat like it was on fire and I started singing, "East Bound and Down!"

I always thought it would be thrilling to ride along with Burt Reynolds (God rest his soul) in that black Trans Am as he and Jerry Reed carried bootleg beer across the country or drive a sports car in the "Cannonball Run" with fellow Ohioan Dean Martin in a caravan race across the country. And here I was thrust into the middle of one traveling through central Indiana having a blast in my Ford Escape!

The caravan kept coming. Everywhere I looked there was a wrapped luxury sports car - in my side mirrors, my rearview mirror, my back window, my side window and front windshield. I was a part of this (in my mind), and the craziest thing was just before this I was really feeling my father's presence with me.

Earlier that morning, I had passed several white Ford Rangers (the kind of truck he had) and multiple big yellow Mac trucks (my dad and I love yellow), and his presence just felt so real. Maybe it was because I was traveling towards the Indy 500 raceway where he and my husband and sons went a long time ago. He would have thought this caravan of rally cars was equally exhilarating.

Burt Reynolds passed away a few months after my father, so his spirit had to be traveling in one of those high-performance cars and without a doubt Steve McQueen was somewhere in the mix. How was I so sure of this? Because the very place where this was happening was close to where Steve was born, St. Francis Hospital in Beech Grove, Indiana. Complete confirmation that the Holy Spirit loves cars and blessing me with special moments on the highway with my father and

Steve McQueen.

The caravan of cars sported Lamborghini, Ferrari, Land Rover, Porsche, Corvette, and others. To maintain my safe driving record, I kept my eyes on the road as best I could and wasn't able to read the multiple sponsors who paid to have their logos on these rapidly moving hypercars. Caught up in the frenzy, I kept myself in the middle of the pack, only after they slowed to the posted speed limit when two had been pulled over by a state trooper.

I don't fully comprehend why I get such an adrenaline rush traveling in a convoy. When I was young and we went camping, there were four families who followed each other in our minivans and campers. I would look behind to make sure they were in tow or look ahead to confirm we were not being left behind, there was something exciting about forging a journey together.

This rally car adventure through flatland Indiana supplied yet another "sign," not one at a shrine or in the clouds or burning bushes. God knows my father loved cars, and Steve McQueen loved cars and racing, and some of my favorite movies include cars and a fun caravan. It was a divine gift to be on that road, at that time, in that exact spot, experiencing that once-in-a-lifetime moment. This was far more spiritual than staring at concrete statues or a waxed woman in a glass box. God was in my car blessing me with an another message that my dad was still with me, this time as my highway navigator.

Later that day, I researched "The Gold Rush Rally," a 100-unit luxury car road rally that stops in 10 cities in 10 days, stays at luxury hotels and makes public appearances. And it's only $20,000 per car to join. I read more. One year, it started in Boston and ended in Vegas, while another time it started in New York City and ended in Miami. This night the race had a scheduled stop at the Indy 500 Raceway for a public appearance. Right where I was heading! My mind was racing as fast as those cars.

Not to disappoint the gift of fate, I finished my calls early, and high tailed it to the raceway that afternoon for a good parking space. There were plenty of spaces and I found the perfect one under a giant poster of a race car driver. I chose a random spot, and when I looked up, I saw a ginormous poster of James Hinchcliff, the six-time champion of the

Indy car series and dancer extraordinaire on "Dancing with the Stars." I recalled how he moved around the ballroom with natural rhythm, talent, and he reminded me of my favorite dancer of all time, the debonaire Fred Astaire. Chills made the hair on my neck stand up.

I thought "What a great team James and I would make in this Gold Rush Rally. We could race by day and dance all night. Sign me up." My bags were packed, and I was ready to follow this caravan wherever they were going.

However, the only place I was going was out of my mind at the timing and correlation of every minute of this special day. After sitting there at the supposed start time and being the only one in the parking lot, I reread the article and realized that I was a year late. The scheduled stop in Indy was the prior year. This year, the route was traveling from Miami to Austin and not stopping in Indy, just passing through on their way to Chicago.

Ergo, I am adding this rally to my bucket list. I will save up my money and with a miracle have a luxury car to drive with a team in this road rally. Or, better yet, I can organize my own road rally, one that is more affordable. Perhaps a classic car caravan starting in Detroit and ending in Miami, or NYC to Hollywood. Or a VW Beetle caravan starting at Woodstock and ending at Berkley with stops in hippie towns like Yellow Springs, Ohio along the way. Or since it is important to keep cars' mileage to a minimum, I could coordinate a rally where people joined along the road, sort of like a conga line. Drivers could come in and out as they please, like I did today, participating in the thrill but keeping distance and monetary commitment low.

If the Lord is willing, and the classic car angels in heaven oversee my dream, then I'm doing the rally with James Hinchcliffe as my co-driver by day, dance partner by night or perhaps my husband or sons or daughter. I am not certain who will be the lucky one to ride with me, but I am certain that my dad, Steve, and St. Francesca Romana (patron saint of drivers) will be our Guardian Angels.

33

*"The true work of art is but a shadow
of the divine perfection."*

Michelangelo
Italian Artist, Architect, Poet

On yet another seemingly ordinary day, this one with an innocent trip to the craft store, my spiritual holy fruit was picked, tested, pressed down, and squeezed out. The experience was less exhilarating and more humiliating.

For my birthday, I bought myself a bold and colorful 8x10 print, a special print that needed the perfect frame. Not too expensive, but not too inexpensive like the metal ones from the corner drug store. The print itself was only $25. Far be it from me to spend too much money on something of little monetary value with a professional frame. Yet, the print had a very personal meaning and deserved a quality frame and nice border.

I did not, do not, nor ever will have, an eye for color, especially when it comes to decorating. It can be excruciatingly confusing and time consuming when choosing the right color for walls, a front door, clothes, hair dye, etc. No matter how much time spent looking at hundreds of paint samples, clothing options, or pieces of hair, I never get it right on the first try.

Thankfully, I am exceptional when it comes to choosing the perfect picture frame. Honestly, I have never disappointed myself with a frame decision. Looking around at any picture in my house, I smile with complete confidence at every frame chosen. The struggle lies in making the correct choice for the matting because of my ineptitude over color. Deciding between a hue in my favorite color pallet or pulling one from something within the picture is a true dilemma.

This print was more challenging than any other one I had ever framed; it was full of bold multi-colors, and I wrestled with which color to highlight. I thought since there were so many different colors in it, the border needed to be neutral to let the subject of the print pop. I envisioned getting a frame that appeared to be distressed wood, maybe with some marks in it.

My arduous journey began when my daughter and I arrived at the local craft store where they sold frames off the rack and offered semi-professional framing. She went in one direction to look at something, and my path led straight to the picture framing section.

While searching every shelf from top to bottom, the kind of wooden frame matching my vision for this piece did not exist. There were many options of size, color, texture, and quality but just not *the one* in my head. There was no one standing at the workstation counter to help me. Then I saw a woman abruptly turn around and walk away through the employee work room door just as I approached the large desk where qualified employees help customers like me make good decisions.

I stood for a little while expecting her to return to the counter, assuming she saw me approaching before she twirled in the opposite direction. Maybe she did and maybe she did not, we will never know. After giving her ample time to return to her station and help, she did not re-enter through the doorway.

It made sense to look around a little longer at the selection of ready-made frames on the shelves. Perhaps I missed one that was hidden behind another, or I perused the shelves too hastily the first time around. After giving it my absolute best search, nothing was the right size or completed the vision for this piece as it appeared in my imagination.

Returning to the counter again, I pushed the button for help. After a while, a long while, she reappeared slowly, barely out of the backroom and remained safely against the back wall. Her mouth did not open, her eyes were on me, yet she spoke no words, she only stared at me. I looked at her expecting an offer of help. When my expression failed to bring forth her offer, it was time for me to move along with my agenda explaining the kind of frame I was searching for. Her response, "They are over there." And she pointed to the other side of the store. I explained I already looked "over there" and did not find one in the right size.

She remained in the same position, just looking at me. I stood firm looking at her. Seeing she needed my guidance; I asked this young woman if I could look at some of the wooden frames to possibly have it framed professionally. She semi-nodded and with a limp lift of her hand pointed to hundreds of frame corners behind her. I described what was in my head, her only reaction was lifting her index finger an inch higher in the same backward direction.

Finding myself in as much of a trance as she, I wondered "Is she okay? Is she about to pass out, or just socially awkward?" My daughter was still off looking at something else and not available to help me assess the situation, nor be a witness to this interaction, more accurately lack of interaction.

Concerned, I politely asked this store employee, "Do you want me to come back and pick the ones I want to look at?" She shrugged her shoulders. My concern and patience shifted slightly, and I looked at her as if to say, "Why aren't you helping me with this?!" She looked at me like, "I am not helping you with this." We were getting nowhere at this point, and I did not care if she was shy. She was an employee working in picture frames, getting paid to help me and, frankly, was not doing her job.

I thought maybe if I took my 8x10 print out of my bag she would come closer to the counter and better understand the theme of my print and we would discuss this project. I removed the artwork from my bag and began to explain my confusion over the border color, my inability to choose colors and the need for a specific frame. She stayed back and away from the counter looking like she was about to escape through the threshold again. Clearly, she needed more prompting.

I asked her what her opinion was, because she was trained and would have a professional eye for what would be best. She offered no help, no suggestions, just a cocked confused head tilt. Obviously, she must have come over from the yarn section.

With the print on the table, I became the employee and helped myself by pulling a few of the matte border samples onto the table to see which color looked best. She moved a few steps toward the oversize workstation just enough to see my print. I thought that was progress and hoped she would assist me. I kept searching through the samples, putting several different colors and textures next to my print, nothing matched, my conversation ambled one sided. She was not acting annoyed at me for being a demanding customer, nor did she have an attitude, she just stood there not helping me, not speaking, not offering a professional opinion, nothing.

My print lay on the table, my irritation percolated with a boldness in my voice, a tilt of my head, and determined look on my face I highly encouraged her, "Could you help me with this?" Then she said, "I don't know what you want." My cup runneth over, "I do not know what I want either! But (sweetheart) that is what you are here for, to help me figure it out." It was not registering, she was not receiving my message, my plea for help. Her blank stare was like an empty canvas in the art department.

It was at this moment when my daughter returned to my side, just in time to witness her mother at her best demanding customer self. And it went like this...I looked down at my print surrounded by poor choices of border colors and textures, back up at the clerk, then back down at my print.

Out of complete frustration, and now boiling aggravation, I put my print very angrily back into my bag and declared to this clerk with exaggerated head and hand movements, "YOU ARE THE LEAST HELPFUL PERSON I'VE EVER MET!" That was my subtle hint to get her to do her job, but she did not take my direction, instead she took a step backward.

Exasperated I thought, 'WHAT THE HELL, woman?!' She was not getting it, and I was not getting my print framed. I turned and walked deliberately away in a huff, my daughter followed totally confused and embarrassed. I was taking my Romero Britto "Jesus" print somewhere else to get framed.

Flabbergasted! This store was not close by, and we wasted time and gas to get there. We settled in the car and my daughter started laughing, asking me "What was that about?" Explaining the exchange between the inept clerk and myself to my amused daughter fired me up even more. Then when I angrily shouted the words, "my Jesus print." The irony of my actions over the purchase of a frame for my Prince of Peace extinguished my fire like a bucket of cold water.

What was wrong with her? More like what was wrong with me. I had Jesus in my hand yet acted like the devil trying frame him. I thought maybe I should go back into the store and apologize, but three-quarters of me was still angry with her lack of customer service skills. Sorry to report, I did not go back in to apologize.

The more I thought about our encounter, the more I realized this kind of exchange between two civilized adults was an excellent example of religious hypocrisy. We go to church, study the bible, have scriptures all over our house, cars, billboards, and wear T-shirts and crucifix necklaces, and then lack love, grace, patience, and show no mercy. Oftentimes starting in the parking lot after church and more often with store clerks and others who deal with the public.

I recalled being fired from my first job for not being an aggressive enough salesclerk at Susie's Casuals in the mall. If a customer shopped for a pair of pants, I showed them pants. But the owner wanted me to offer them a shirt, belt, hat, and multiple other accessories too. That wasn't my style of customer service. Possibly, this clerk had her own interpretation of customer service, one of a more laid-back approach as to not interfere with the customer's vision. Another possibility, she may have thought I needed Jesus in my attitude, and not on my wall. And she would be right, regardless of how others act, we own our reactions and if we proclaim to know and love Jesus, then we should act with the same level of grace, patience, and mercy with everyone. Especially toward others working with the public.

34

"We're all born naked, and the rest is drag."

RuPaul
Entertainer, actor, musician

My solace came from knowing the greats of the bible were far from perfect as well. Consider the twelve apostles, they had issues with betrayal, little faith, hard hearts, selfish-ambition, and jealousy. David, the "man after God's own heart" and great king was deceitful, an adulterer, and murderer. Saul, before he was Paul, was the most aggressive persecutor of Christians in history, imprisoning both men and women believers.

I am not categorizing myself as a bible great, but it's good to know even God's most notable were as flawed as the rest of us.

To make myself feel better about my lack of grace and patience, I considered an experience when a "Christian" woman cut me out of her life. Although our church attendance was sporadic, I remained active in her bible study courses. They were never as good as the one with Lydia, nothing ever could be, but I always found something worthwhile about being together with a group of women believers studying God's word.

This woman was retired and frequently invited me via text and email to meet one-on-one. Her goal was to meet once a month, but my personal and professional schedule were barely free for us to meet every few months. When we met, our conversations were light and friendly. I never had an agenda and was naïve enough to think she didn't have one either.

The trouble started when she explained her role in the church was to get people "to do more than just attend church on Sunday." She shockingly expressed "There are some people who only attend one service per weekend, can you imagine?!" Yes, I can imagine. But I didn't respond immediately and let her continue.

She felt every congregant should participate in small groups, various ministries, and other activities sponsored by the church. I didn't agree nor disagree, but her tone was judgmental of those who didn't, and that struck a negative chord in me.

Once she finished, I wasn't sure if her words were directed at me or if she was enlisting my help to increase attendance with other groups and church events. Either way, it didn't sit well with me, and I kindly suggested she pull back her judgment of others lack of attendance and extracurricular activity level. She does not, nor does anyone know of what goes into attending church.

I explained what if someone is a caregiver and only has coverage for a loved one for that one hour on Sunday. Or those with work and family commitments? Or my friend who led the music ministry in her church for 40 years, who now just wants to attend and enjoy the service on Sunday? She was taken aback by my defense of the people who didn't meet her activity standards.

Nor did she understand that for Catholics' church attendance is our main obligation. Growing up and as an adult, I don't recall small groups and certainly no bible studies. Although, now in the Catholic church there are various groups and ministries to join, but historically, involvement in the church was mass, CCD (Sunday school for youth not enrolled in Catholic Schools), and ushering, choir, and financial support - all done at or during mass.

Being a perceptive woman, she changed the subject and asked about my job. This was the clincher. When I explained my product was to treat HIV and my support for the LGBTQ community including colleagues, friends, and family, her painted upper lip curled. Then she asked if HIV was even still a thing and "have you been able to change them or are those people still like that?"

The more she carried on about "those people," I thought of a scripture I once read about the church leaving the judgment to God and concentrating on setting its own house in order. It hurts my heart when people speak of being angry at God because of the way "Christians" point their finger in judgement. There are churches that state a dress code, ostracize the LGBTQ+ community, disrespect divorced people, and look at those with tattoos with great disdain. It's wrong. They aren't God and aren't representing divine love when treating people with contempt. Only God can vet heaven, and it's wrong to use the bible to hate, dislike, or ostricize another creation of God. Only God knows our hearts and the after life.

Sensing another layer of judgement from this church thought leader, it was time to enlighten her with the wisdom Father John shared with me twenty years ago, "to love God first, and to love each other second." That's all, if all humans did just those two things this world would be full of peace, love, and joy.

She squirmed in her padded booth seat, pursed her perfectly red lipstick lips, and had no rebuttal. Quoting scripture, and the most important words from the living word of the most holy bible, what could she say? She looked at her watch, and said she had to go.

After that coffee conversation, I never received another text, email, bible study, or women's ministry invite again. She unfriended me. Cut me off because I stood up for people whom she knew nothing about and could only see through her judging eyes. Honestly, I prefer the company of a divorced, gay, tattooed person dressed in rags over a narrow-minded nincompoop.

35

"For You will not abandon my soul to Sheol"

Psalm 16:10 ESV

My father-in-law was a devout Catholic, Fourth Degree Knights of Columbus, he recited the Chaplet of Divine Mercy at 3 a.m. and 3 p.m., and religiously attended daily Mass, weekend services, adorations, etc. There was never a more committed man to Catholicism. And he called *me* sunshine, the man knew a bright spirit when he saw one.

A few years ago, he was diagnosed with pulmonary fibrosis, and due to this disease, struggled for every breath. He defied all medical odds as he squeezed every ounce of oxygen with quick and miniscule puffs of air.

During one of our chairside chats, I asked him about some of his fondest memories. We ended up talking about classic automobiles and he told me his favorite was the 1959 Cadillac, then asked me if I knew why. I had no idea, he explained it was the year with the highest tailfins, then he laughed. This vision prompted an idea which I brought to fruition and blessed me with a memory I will never forget.

I set out to find someone who owned a 1959 Cadillac and would be willing to take my father-in-law cruisin' or, at the very least, drive by the house. It wasn't easy, but with enough digging around, I made a connection through the local car club. After many phone calls and insistence on this specific Cadillac, a wonderful woman, Gloria, came through with her white 1959 Cadillac with red leather interior willing to take my father-in-law through the town and neighborhood. Seeing my in-laws in the front seat smiling at each other as if teenagers in love filled my heart. We rode around like movie stars with class and style. People smiled and waved as we passed by in this classic work of art. The joy in that ride was unmistakable and unforgettable.

When his condition worsened, and he became housebound, he fully accepted his physical limitations and suffering as a way of giving glory to God. He considered it an opportunity to develop grace and mercy regarding his own situation and toward others. His sense of humor never faded, nor did his faith in a miracle, Mother Mary, and whatever fate God had for his life.

Out of respect to him and our relationship, I never challenged him about his religious beliefs that I found unbiblical. I listened without agreeing or disagreeing to keep the peace, but more so, I refused to let a confrontation be our last conversation. And yet, not being a biblical scholar myself, it was imperative for me to seek the truth of his strong convictions for Catholicism.

It wasn't a pursuit of being right to satisfy my own pride, it was an internal curiosity. Whenever I heard something that didn't sit well with me, my prayer and meditations became inquisitive, asking God, "is that true?"

During one morning walk when I asked that question again, the Holy Spirit responded with a clarifying question followed by a clear plan. Was I sincerely interested in the truth? If yes, then I needed to spend time alone, one word at a time led by the living word. Just God and I, me and the Divine, no middleman, no TV evangelist prophesying scripture, no radio pastor preaching the Gospel according to himself, no priest pontificating a decade-old homily, only me and the Creator.

I was delighted to receive a clear and simple response, and planned to light a candle, sit in silence and solitude, and read one word at a time in alphabetical order from the concordance. This is not the recommended way of reading the bible, it was just a personal prompt that spoke to me. One would never read a book one random word or sentence at a time, the story wouldn't make sense, same with the bible.

I had come to consider the bible like a local independent bookstore, owned by Jesus and ran by his holy staff with various sections for history, poetry, true crime, genealogy, mystery, and inspiration. A safe and sacred place where discussion, discovery, connection, and "a ha!" moments flourish, and all are welcome day and night, with our without shirt and shoes.

I started the project motivated by wanting a better understanding of how the teachings of Catholicism aligned with God's word. I was as determined to find the truth as when seeking that '59 Cadillac, therefore I went directly to the Source. I thanked the Lord God Almighty for all that I had learned so far and for the succinct directions.

It was the end of April when I decided to embark on my "one word a day" project and I would begin on May 1st. Thinking the month of May was a good lead into my personal project and a positive omen considering so many phrases begin with "May…May Thee, May Thou, May God, May you."

It's hard to fully comprehend and explain my gut feelings. Yet when I listen and follow the prompt of my inner voice, I find serendipitous connections abound. There is no one formula to bring forth such encounters, it's about listening to my authentic self, having an open heart and mind, acknowledging and being grateful for the creator's constant presence and being present to the moment.

I had no idea what the first word was in my concordance, but it did not matter because my plan was to start with it anyway. The lead bible for this project was a compact English Standard Version, chosen for practical travel-size purposes and the fewest words listed. I was not being lazy or opting for the Cliff Notes version of my deeper dive, it just made sense to start with one that could accompany me anywhere.

To be fair, and in my defense, I looked at the concordance in all five of my full-size ones to see what word was listed first and they all started with names. When I felt called to do this one-word project, I opened my compact-size one which started with the verb, "abandon" and I knew that was the perfect place and mindset to start, with abandon.

I assumed the scripture would tell me to abandon my old self, my sinful ways, foul language, road rage, and all my other imperfections. That makes total sense. To know God, we must abandon and empty ourselves completely to fully seek the Divine. It is written that when we empty ourselves, then and only then can God fill us.

It was a few days before May 1st when I got the brilliant idea to do this study, so I had several days to contemplate and prepare myself for everything I would be abandoning. I mulled over the act of releasing anything and everything to know the Divine as much as humanly possible.

Then came May 1, opening day of my one-word journey beginning with "abandon." Psalm 16:10 ESV, "I will not abandon your soul to Sheol." My body became one with the chair, my jaw dropped as my soul celebrated. What did the Lord just say directly to me on this first day of our one-word journey?! My spirit leapt and a smile spread so wide across my face it was as if my long-lost dog returned home. It was not about selling my possessions or leaving my well-paying job or leaving my family to become a nun, it was not about me abandoning anything, it was God's promise to *not* abandon *me!*

My whole spiritual focus, since childhood, was about being good enough to get into heaven and not bad enough to end up in hell. My eternal fate, once confirmed by a cheap magazine psyche test in college, made me psychotic about my final destination every day thereafter, and was all for naught! My sense of eternal doom, fire and brimstone, thrashing, pain, punishment, gone with one word. It was as if God himself said, "I need to get something straight with you right from the get-go, I will not abandon your soul to Hell. Got that?! Good, I'm tired of you vacillating between heaven and hell, now let's move on."

I cross-referenced the verse with my full-size bibles just to make sure it was consistent. My Life Principles Bible NKJV said, "For You will not leave my soul in Sheol…" In my Women of Faith Study Bible NIV, "…you will not abandon me to the grave…" My NIV Study Bible repeated, "…you will not abandon me to the grave…" finally in my Ryrie Study Bible Expanded Edition NAS Red Letter Bible, "…For you will not abandon my soul to Sheol…"

To be completely transparent, I had to look up Sheol to be certain it was Hell. I learned it is the Greek version of Hades, which is the Hebrew version of Sheol, and Hell is the universal version of Sheol. Hades is the place of dreaded darkness where the dead go.

Every version corroborated with the other. Reading Psalm 16:10, every version, over and over peeled away decades of delusion about having an advance ticket to the lake of fire. If the scripture was not enough of a wow factor, it was multiplied by the timing of it as the first word of this divinely inspired project. The Divine made it unique by starting with something that consumed me my entire life.

I experienced a complete calm wash over me and an elated level of gratitude for being special enough for God to answer with such unique specificity to me. I had been like Atlas who held the weight of the under world on my shoulders and then with one simple and holy word was given the strength and freedom to hurl it into the atmosphere. Heavy burden: gone.

What made me so worthy? His word says, because God created me, I am a child of the Divine and loved. This one-word project solidified and rewarded me for listening to my gut and the gentle prompting of the Spirit. God was in the midst and my heart.

I could not wait to see where this daily word project would take me, and my new-found confidence told me wherever it was, would be far from hell, Hades, and Sheol.

36

*"I would rather be a rider for a minute,
than a spectator for a lifetime."*

Unknown motorcycle enthusiast
(and my father)

My son's fiancé asked him if his grandmother, my mom, had any of my father's T-shirts from Youngstown Cycle, a place where my dad used to work part-time after retiring. She thought they were cool and a little badass with a snake logo. I was with my mom when the conversation happened over text between my son and my mother.

Unfortunately, my mom already made those T-shirts into pillows, but she quickly volunteered to go shopping and purchase one for her. I offered to get it since I was in town helping with my father-in-law, but my mom admitted she wanted to check out the place, it had been a while since she was there.

A few days passed, and while spending time with my mom, she said she got the shirt at the cycle shop and explained, when she went to pay for it, there was a teal blue Cushman Scooter parked in front of the counter. She recognized the seat and style of the motorcycle and asked the man behind the counter if it was once yellow. He said yes and asked her how she knew. She told him, "I think this used to be my husband's scooter" and she asked him where he got it.

He told my mom that the mechanic finished building it in the basement of the store, but it once belonged to the previous owner of the shop. He said he remembered her husband and some of the parts being yellow. My mom knew at that moment it was the one my father was building before he passed.

She confessed that she wanted to buy it and when she came home, she called one of my dad's motorcycle buddies to ask him about the scooter. He discouraged her from making the purchase, reminding her that she does not ride motorcycles, and questioned what she would do with it? It would only sit in her garage with his other motorcycle and it did not make sense to get it. My mom really wanted it, but she was and is a practical person and knew purchasing it was not a practical decision. She knew he was right, she would never ride it, it's a hairdo thing.

She wanted the scooter because it was the last project that mattered to my dad. His hands touched it and worked on it before he became seriously ill. She remembered their trip to North Carolina to get parts, specifically that seat, from a store with hundreds of Cushman scooters where my dad saw the exact one he planned to replicate. She took his picture with the scooter from every angle to ensure his final project matched the one in the showroom. But it was not to be.

When we were talking, I saw the pain in her eyes. She was in the process, very slowly, of clearing out excess clutter in the house and garage and making this purchase would only deter her progress.

She expressed a few more times how much she wanted it because just thinking about my dad in his garage restoring it made her heart ache for my dad's presence. I decided to make time that week to go into the cycle shop and see my dad's final project.

Later that evening, when I was alone, I perused the internet for late 1950s Cushman scooters. Before seeing any image, I pictured a fun sporty Vespa scooter. My dad once owned two and I pictured Audrey Hepburn riding one with glee in "Roman Holiday." But when the images came up, I gagged and thought those are ugly! Most of them had a slanted metal box over the back tire, like an industrial size weirdly shaped mailbox. A far cry from a cute Vespa in my head, they were hideous.

However, I too wanted to see with my own eyes something my dad had worked on, even if it was weird looking. The next morning, my calendar unexpectedly cleared and I was free to enjoy a few hours alone. I decided to have a cup of coffee with my dad and take my on-line meditation class at his gravesite to connect with him over much needed quiet time.

I purchased a honey vanilla latte, drove to the cemetery, took out my yoga mat, placed it next to his headstone where I read his name, life dates, and saw the engraved motorcycle below his name. On the same stone is my mom's name, no ending date, and a classic Crown Victoria below her name, the kind they had when they were first married. Centered between their names was an attached bronze vase for flowers, reminding me of how solid and secure their marriage was from the beginning until the end.

I sat and talked with my dad while drinking my coffee, then meditated with my online class. His gravesite welcomed contemplation and meditation thanks to the cherry blossom tree my mom planted at the foot of his grave. The tree-lined cemetery created a natural protective wall around the flat grave markers. His final resting place was well cared for and relatively quiet for its location between two main roads.

While following along with the meditations, I tried not to let my mind wander and my heart weigh too heavy with grief and regret. I should have been a better daughter to this wonderful man. I could not stop the barrage of negative thoughts taking my mind captive and traveling down Horrible Daughter Lane. I lived my life with me at the center, and once I started having children, they became the center of my world. I loved them more than life itself and every minute was spent focused on whatever they needed.

As I sat at my dad's grave, my head hurt from holding back tears. I was such a fool, if only I could tell my dad how sorry I was for not giving him more time, respect, love, and mercy.

I did not know what life was like for him growing up on a farm with numerous siblings, a mother with potentially mental illness and a grandmother who chewed tobacco and could be meaner than an angry goat. I believe now that he did his best. He was one of the greatest men I will ever know and was wonderful to so many people, including me. I could not tell him in this world how deeply sorry I was that he was gone.

Halfway through my meditation class it started to rain, real rain drops on my head in addition to the stream pouring from my tear ducts. I finished meditating in my car.

Class was over, my latte finished, and my heart ripped to shreds. It made perfect sense to go see the scooter at the cycle shop, it would either add balm or salt to my open wound. I owed it to my father to take the time and see it, just like when he invited me to his garage to "check this out." I fully regret not accepting all his garage invitations with more enthusiasm and less irritation. I hoped he was watching me at this moment and saw me going to see something that mattered to him, and he understood this small gesture was my way of apologizing for being such a brat.

Youngstown Cycle was just down the street from the cemetery, and it probably was my dad's second favorite place. He loved being around motorcycles, talking about them, riding them, and re-building them, so that probably was not the hardest job he ever had.

Walking into the store, I looked right at the counter where my mom said the scooter was and did not see anything. I asked the man behind the counter, "Did you have a blue scooter here the other day?" He looked at me funny and asked, "Do you know Pat?" I smiled and explained that I was her daughter, and with those words, my eyes released the flood. While barely speaking, mostly sobbing, and constant sniffling, I explained that scooter was my father's last project.

The man, unsure how to handle this unexpected and highly emotional situation, described where it was and pointed toward its location in the center of the store. I turned, and there it was. The cutest little motorcycle I ever saw. It was not ugly at all. It was not mail boxy; it was a real motorcycle, and it was just my size. Oh my heart. Three weeks prior, I was given a Yeti type water jug the exact same color and two days prior to this moment I bought a blender bottle in this very color of blue. My father's scooter was the same "ocean mist" light blue. I love the ocean, and this was the third time this exact color came to me. This hue of blue was uniquely authentic to the 1950s and spoke to me in this serendipitous moment.

Tears clouded my vision as I could not take my eyes off it. I gently touched it and pictured my dad working on it. The man came out from behind the counter and asked if I wanted to start it up. I did not know engines could be started inside buildings. He explained, "It's a blast to ride, we ride it all the time around here. Do you want to take it for a ride?"

He assumed I knew how to ride motorcycles. Little did he know, I only rode twice in my life, once on the back of my boyfriend's borrowed minibike, when I was young, stupid, carefree and in love. The second was with my son on my father's bike the day of his funeral. The friendly and helpful man turned out to be the current owner of the store, and said it was easy to start and ride. But I explained I did not want to ride it, I just wanted to see it.

My eyes were glued to this magnificent machine, from every angle, the fenders, the handlebars, the vintage tail fins. It reminded me of a 1950s classic car with detailed designs, and it was nothing at all what I expected.

The owner encouraged me to sit on it. Without thinking twice, I took hold of the handlebars, threw my leg over with ease, and found the seat as comfortable as my favorite leather chair. The seat was oversized, a perfect fit for my derriere, and bouncy, and my arms reached the handlebars as if it were custom made just for me. Holding the dirty white grips on the steel handlebars sent a surge of melancholy through me as I pictured my dad's vision to be on this finished project. His presence was powerful and finding this scooter was not a coincidence. It felt very natural to be on it, and maybe I could ride it.

It was little enough for me to handle, seemed harmless and an antique. I knew at that moment it needed to be in our family. It was Mother's Day weekend and I wanted to get this for my mom, to be able to give her something that meant so much to my dad would mean everything to her. The owner asked the man who finished restoring it to come out from the back to meet me and tell me about the scooter. Ironically, that gentleman's name was the same as my son, the one who had his own motorcycle, rode with my dad, and the one my father asked about on his last morning with us.

We talked for a while. He said, "Your dad kept bringing me parts in boxes." He explained to me the details of rebuilding each part and the shared conversations he had with my dad about the bike. Everything in me said, "BUY IT!", but I hear that voice a lot, especially in the shoe department.

The words came out of my mouth quickly and confidently, "I want to buy it." And I did, along with a matching ocean-mist helmet and

I promised to return the following week to complete the transaction. They asked if I had a trailer. Shaking my head, I said, "Nope. I will be riding it home." They liked that idea, not having any clue that I never drove a motorcycle before.

37

"Live dangerously. Take the whole day."

Gregory Peck
Roman Holiday

That evening while keeping company with my mom watching television, I told her I stopped by the cycle shop to see dad's scooter. Her face lit up, "Wasn't that neat?" Her smile stretched from ear to ear. Seeing her elation, I blurted, "I bought it for you for Mother's Day." She screamed, her jaw dropped, and I saw on her face how full her heart was. She could not believe it and was thrilled, speechless, and rivers flowed down both our cheeks.

She called everyone she knew the next day to tell them about it. I knew by her reaction that I made a very practical and purposeful purchase.

Another source pushing my impulsive decision was the decline in my father-in-law's health. The past few years were true examples of how short life can be and the need to live it to the fullest. Shortly after my scooter purchase, he passed. His condition declined where he fought for every breath, until the last one took him home. While my father's illness and death were quick and unexpected, his was slow and anticipated for several years.

After the funeral and life calmed down, I focused on getting my dad's scooter home to my mom. The how wasn't clear yet, but my imagination was percolating a plan.

The following days my mind went overboard with a master plan for this sentimental motorcycle. I would sign up for motorcycle lessons, get my license, and ride it home myself. When I told my son, the one with his own motorcycle, he fully supported my plan and said he would like to ride along with me. Perfect.

My mom told my dad's friends and they wanted to ride along too. This was going to be extraordinary. I had just enough time to read the manual and take the written exam to bring my dad's bike home on the perfect day, Father's Day weekend.

I went back to the cycle shop to practice riding the scooter and told the owner that my son wanted to ride my dad's Royal Enfield Bullet motorcycle to escort me home. And a few of my father's riding buddies would join too. He asked, "Can my father and I be a part of that too, if that's okay?" Totally! Then, adding to my plans, he asked if he could extend the invitation to his customers, other employees, and friends to join with their fathers. The excitement grew exponentially.

He fired it up in the store for me to ride around outside in the neighboring church parking lot. As soon as I sat on the seat, motor purring, hands gripping the handlebars, feeling the vibration of this unique antique machine, adrenaline rushed through my entire body, it was invigorating. I immediately transformed into a biker chick. I would never be the same non-motorcycle woman ever again. I could ride it. I was riding it, and the excitement and freedom and badassery of doing it was intoxicating.

I just needed practice, and a major cup of courage. And later found out - a motorcycle license, written and riding tests, a motorcycle riding course, insurance, a bill of sale, a title, and a license plate. I don't always think through the thoughts I think.

I downloaded the motorcycle manual for the test and, it was bad, very bad. The whole book was about crashes: how to avoid them, how to expect and survive when (not if) they happened, fatalities, severe injuries, every intersection is potentially fatal, and everything that could and will go wrong with the cycle while in motion. I was in way over my head, but I had to have my dad's motorcycle for my mom. The more I studied, the more horrific scenarios fed my fear.

The owner of the cycle shop had commitments from several customers and employees who wanted to take part. This was going to be a magnificent event and I needed to gather my courage, get my license and more importantly, purchase an outfit. I could not back out now.

The day came to ride my father's scooter home. I had not slept well all week; it was a combination of excitement of bringing it home where it belonged and being frightened with worry about wrecking it, or seeing my son wreck, or all of us wrecking. I barely passed the written test, on the second attempt. I bought a super cute, but safe, outfit including a brown leather jacket, matching gloves, white jeans, sturdy Timberland work boots, cute hot pink sweater tank top, and "Peace, Love, and Sunshine" stickers for my helmet. I thought more about my outfit than I did about the responsibility and dangers of riding a motorcycle on an actual road.

Father's Day weekend arrived, and we were bringing it home. Me, on the scooter, my son on my dad's bike, two of my father's best friends on their motorcycles, the owner of the shop and his dad and a band of Harley's escorting us to my parent's house. I was thrilled and scared out of my wits. The young man behind the counter said, "The most important thing you can do is breathe." I asked, "Can you tell I am not breathing?!" He smiled and nodded his head..

I tried to start it, but I could not, it was the kind where I had to jump with all my strength and weight on the metal thing. The owner started it for me and I took it around the church parking lot a few times to get my nerves to settle and say some major prayers.

It was one of the most exhilarating experiences of my life. Witnessed by more than twenty family and friends and people I never met gathered to share this momentous event of escorting my dad's 1959 Cushman Eagle home.

It was a sight to be seen; me, with my matching ocean blue mist helmet, being half-badass and half-geek, riding this antique motorcycle through the streets, surrounded by loud rumbling Harley Davidson motorcycles.

The Harley riders made a protective wall for me to be the first onto the road and it was sheer terror! I kept my eye on my son who took the lead, then the owner of the cycle shop, God bless him, never left my side. He was riding close enough to protect me and yet far enough away to be safe.

Our plan was to go through the cemetery first to pass by my father's gravesite, then parade home to my parent's house. I planned to wave and look over at my dad's space, but once my hands were death-gripped on the handlebars, I could not release my fingers to lift my hand.

I felt like I was soaring down the road, breaking the speed limit of 35 miles per hour, going at least 40 to 50 miles per hour. In actuality, and from eyewitnesses around me, I did not ride faster than 20 miles per hour.

I looked in my rearview mirror and saw my entourage. I felt my father's spirit, I felt wild, courageous, and I felt Steve McQueen with me. But I also felt if I did not pay attention to the road I was going to die.

It was energizing and heartwarming and all the angels (not Hell's, but heaven's) were with me, including my grandmother. I was reminded later that very day was the anniversary of my grandmother's passing. Thank the Good Lord for not having our deaths be on the same date.

This parade honored my dad and my mom. I rode his scooter to their house, to my father's garage where his hands worked on it, his mind envisioned it, and his passion started it. It and I were safely home. We celebrated with a pizza party in the front yard for all.

Every time I went to visit my mom, I started it up. The sound of it made me feel like a real motorcycle momma. I rode it around, not too far, once over to my in-laws two miles away, but starting it was harder than opening a jar of pickles. I hit my leg on some part sticking out so severely once I had a hematoma the size of a golf ball on my shin. I never rode with confidence; my plan was to ride in parades and go to Cushman gatherings.

My imagination went wild once and thought about starting a "Skirts on Scooters Club." A riding club just for women; we would wear outfits from the year of our scooters. I got such a thrill picturing my motorcycle club of female vintage fashion riders. I searched online to see if one existed and to my surprise and disappointment there were several attempts for all female riding clubs, but none with much success, nor vintage attire.

The last time I rode the cycle it was one weekend with just my mom and me. It took several if not one hundred attempts to start it. I had no intention of riding it, but the scooter needed to be started as often as possible for good antique motorcycle maintenance. I questioned if maybe my father was somehow preventing me from starting it on purpose and perhaps did not want me on the roads. Anyhow, it eventually started but I was not wearing my safety gear, so I only planned to start it and listen to the engine.

As soon as it started, I had to sit on it, and when I sat on it, I had to ride it. I went to the end of the driveway. It was dusk. I turned around and asked my mom to take my picture. I wanted one like Audrey Hepburn on her scooter in "Roman Holiday." In my irresponsible excitement and desire for the perfect picture, I forgot how to use the brakes. I was focused on starting it and smiling for the camera, my mind blanked on how to stop.

I traveled rapidly down the driveway and screamed because it sped faster as I approached the garage. I kept twisting the handle engaging the throttle thrusting the bike forward. I thought twisting the handle would make it stop, but it only made the engine work more. I had no clue how to brake, so I turned the handlebars to the left to avoid crashing into the garage and my mom's van, all the while hoping my screaming would stop the forward motion. It did not.

I ended up in the backyard and slammed into the back patio, flowerpots, and fire pit. It was a hard stop into the railing posts. The front of the scooter was damaged as well as the slats of the patio railing and everything in my path. At least it stopped moving and surprisingly I remained upright, albeit shaken upright. My hands were trembling when I turned off the engine, while my mom met me in the backyard, not knowing what to expect. After we examined the bike and her porch for damage, we felt it best not to ride the cycle until I knew how to use the brakes. And no, she did not capture my gleeful or horrified expression while riding my scooter.

I was deeply grateful to be unharmed and that it happened in my parent's back yard. Angels watched over me, offering protection and a gentle reminder that I was no Audrey Hepburn.

38

"The future of life on Earth depends on our ability to see the sacred where others see only the common."

John Denver
Singer, Songwriter, Musician,
Actor, Activist, Poet, Humanitarian

The following month, on September 8th, two days before what would have been my father's 82nd birthday, I was making sales calls from Piketon, Ohio, to Parkersburg, West Virginia. This also happens to be the region where my father's ancestors settled. Of course, he and his kinfolk were on my mind. The exceptionally scenic drive featured multi-colored rock formations on both sides of the freeway, allowing an opportunity to appreciate the beauty and awe of nature. The sun was high in the blue sky, and I was overcome with gratitude for the countless blessings in my life of good health, family, friends, and my job which included the ability to travel, provide life-saving medicine, and my brand-new Chevy Equinox company car.

This second time around in pharmaceutical sales was different. I had changed, and of greater significance, the industry had changed. During the eight years that I was in the senior care field, there was a complete overhaul of regulations and guidelines among pharmaceutical companies, patient's rights, hospitals, and clinicians. No more lavish dinners or promotional items including pens, nor any form of entertainment.

The strict guidelines were a welcome change and, being with a small company, it felt more like a family who respected my gifts and talents. I most appreciated their high level of standards and ethics. This position and my manager came along at the right time with an opportunity for me to develop personally and professionally. I was grateful to be back in the revised edition of the industry.

I had been listening to an audio book during the long drive, but decided to take a break since I became preoccupied with the beauty and blessings surrounding me and not on the subject matter of the latest self-help book. I turned on the radio to add a musical soundtrack to my driving experience.

However, the only station that came in clear was the Catholic station. It was the beginning of the program called Point of Grace. The very program that my father-in-law highly recommended that I watch on television, but it was on at 11 p.m., which was way past my preferred bedtime. I never watched it or listened to the program before, and this felt like the right time to give it a chance. Imagine my surprise when the announcers mentioned that very day was Mother Mary's birthday, I nearly ran off the road. My father-in-law adored and honored the Blessed Mother.

Today of all days this was the program's focus, and they asked the listening audience if they had recently lost a loved one whom they wanted to pray for in purgatory. I thought about my father-in-law and my father, I did not think either of them were in purgatory, nor do I think purgatory exists. But I appreciated the reminder to hold them in my heart and prayers at that moment.

As any cautious and attentive driver does regularly, I look from side to side, and when I looked to my right there was a sign for Our Lady of Fatima Shrine. I was having another providential "pinch me please" encounter where heaven and the spirit of a loved one surrounds me from every angle reminding me of their love and eternal presence.

Our Lady of Fatima was the place in Portugal where the Blessed Mother appeared to three young children on six different occasions. That significant event meant the world to my father-in-law and the fact that I was passing by this specific shrine, while listening to his favorite program, on the Blessed Mother's birthday blew my finite mind.

Moments like these can only be orchestrated by a higher power with infinite knowledge. It was yet another specially designed sign reminding me that the space between heaven and earth is thinner than air.

These personal messages almost always happen outside of church. I am not alone in these outside of church experiences, consider Moses' burning bush, Saul walking on the road to Damascus, Mary in her own home, Jonah in the whale or Noah in his workshop. And my personal favorite, Sister Faustina who encountered Jesus while on the dance floor in a nightclub. From one dancing queen to another, she's my kind of mystic.

I will never forget the night in my bedroom with a classic movie, or the many events while in my car, or countless connections with nature. The list keeps growing. My real point is that God is ever present and available to all with childlike faith. Most of my divine encounters appear when I: meditate on God's word, am outside of a church building, in a constant conversation with the Divine, and willing to be called an hysteric, as Saint Faustina once was for sharing her encounter with Jesus.

I feel God's presence and direction most intensely when my mind is open and heart softened, often broken, or needs breaking. For instance, one day I was giving my husband an ear full. I was right about every issue in the case I presented against his opinion. I knew I was right and I did not back down, he also knew it and apologized with every point I made.

As soon as I ended my diatribe, I turned on my high horse and walked away to finish my daily devotional time. I opened my devotional book and voila… right in my face, forgiveness, and the need to forgive and to be forgiven. It explained, God forgives us and expects us to do the same. We all need forgiveness from others throughout our lives, so we must also be forgiving of others who have wronged us. Every time, every stinkin' time, my pride fluffs my peacock feathers, the Lord reminds me "to remove the log in my own eye before removing the stick in someone else's eye." (Matthew 7:5 ESV)

After more than 30 years of marriage to my high school sweetheart, the biggest secret to a happy marriage is forgiveness, the giving of it and accepting it with love and respect. A happy marriage is not about communication, it is not through a man's stomach, and it is not playing games in the bedroom with costumes, nor keeping a designated date night. Nothing else saves relationships more than forgiveness.

A forgiving spirit must be one of the most important spiritual characteristics when we consider it was the final act of grace Jesus offered before his death on the cross. He forgave the man next to him of his sins and he forgave the crowd who brutally beat and crucified him. Clearly, those actions are strong endorsements for how important forgiveness is to God.

39

"There is not a tree in Heaven that is higher than the tree of patience."

Irish Proverb

After my father's passing, our neighbors were kind enough to give me a gift card to the local outdoor nursery. It was a generous and thoughtful way to honor my dad with a tree in our yard. He enjoyed caring for the landscape of his own house and always mentioned how pretty our flowering crabapple tree was in our front yard. He appreciated the beauty and work involved with maintaining flowers and trees. It must have been from his farming genes and Celtic ancestry.

I waited for my mom to visit, and on her first solo trip without my father, we went to the nursery to choose a tree or flowering plant my father would have enjoyed. We looked at several options, however I have minimal expertise of the species or the sun, water, and soil requirements to grow anything. My appreciation runs deep for those with botanical knowledge and the ability to maintain vegetation.

After much discussion with an employee and examining every tree, we decided on a magnolia tree. It is considered an evergreen because it keeps its leaves year around, although it doesn't look like a pine tree that I associate with an evergreen. The tree was supposed to get white flowers and be hearty enough to flourish in Ohio weather. This was fall, and it didn't have flowers at that time, but we brought the solid tree home and planted it near the patio in our backyard where I could see it every day from my kitchen window, the place I spent most of my waking hours.

We didn't research the tree or ask for more details. We knew it would do well in my full sun backyard, my mom picked it and knew my dad would like it. Then the following mid-June, Father's Day weekend, the first flower bloomed. What a beautiful message from heaven from my father and the Almighty Creator. The extra divine blessing is that each year this tree begins to bloom on Father's Day, and is in full bloom at the end of June, on the anniversary of his death.

When we chose this tree, we had no idea of when flowers would blossom. The gift of hearty white flowers during those few weeks of the year is a perfect example of the Celtic connection with our ancestors through nature. Yet another reminder of my deep Irish roots and God's constant presence.

Divine timing and intervention continued with the most unexpected and glorious of experiences. Three years after my father passed, our sons married. Two completely opposite ceremonies and courtships. One married in an historic Greek church with an hour-long ceremony and a priest presiding. The other wedding was outdoors in the mountains of North Carolina lasting 20 minutes presided by my first daughter-in-law. My one son dated his bride for almost nine years. We knew everything about her, including her family, friends, special interests, and with living in the same town, we saw her often. The other son met his bride after he moved to another state. They dated barely a year; we saw her a few times and then came the wedding.

It is said that the mother of the groom is to show up and wear beige. However, that's not my style. I wanted to give a speech at the rehearsal dinner, technically the groom's parents' party (MY party) to welcome the women into our family. My first son's wedding was with the bride I knew best. It was easy to write about her because I knew her as well as any future mother-in-law could possibly know. She was a dynamo female role model for my daughter and anyone fortunate to know her.

I wrote the speech in one sitting, and it flowed like a river from head to pen.

With the next wedding, a few months later, my speech was a struggle. Not because of my feelings toward the bride, but because I barely knew her. When thinking about welcoming her to the family, my words focused on her professional career. My quandary was how to deliver a speech without it sounding like her resume before a symposium of her peers.

This toiled around in my mind for weeks on end.

The Tuesday before the wedding I had to be in Columbus to schedule a lunch with a physician's office at 7 a.m., leaving my house at 5:30 a.m., awakening from my slumber at 4:30 a.m. After securing the coveted lunch appointment, I had at least an hour and a half to spare before other offices opened, thus a dilemma - go to breakfast or go to mass. I like checking out various churches when traveling and attending an extra service during the week could be beneficial, especially when something as big as a son's wedding was impending.

I went back and forth between mass or eggs, church or pancakes. It was tough, I am always up for breakfast, and it was only Tuesday, missing mass is only a sin on Sunday. I opted for breakfast.

I drove past a new breakfast restaurant and decided to try it out with the assumption it is extremely difficult to mess up breakfast food. I entered the front door hungry, optimistic, and guilt-free.

Immediately, I was disappointed that I had to go to a counter to order and it was not a "sit down and serve me" kind of place. Okay. I take my time to read the menu, really take my time, then I begin to share my order with the woman behind the counter. She was patient with my lengthy decision time because I was the only customer. As soon as I began to give her my order, she interrupted me with a question about being unfamiliar with the ordering process.

Confused, I assumed telling her would place my order. Not so. She explained that I had to go to the kiosk at the front of the restaurant, place my order, then come back to the counter to pick up my food then find a seat in the dining room.

I was fine with that, until the kiosk system was more complicated than my foggy brain on little sleep could handle, and the food substitutions were limited. I was not about to learn a new skill set to order an egg sandwich. I left.

Feeling a spiritual tug, I looked up the website for mass times near me and found a church not close but in an area of town that I knew. And I liked the name, "Our Lady of Victory."

And thought to myself, I want to be a lady of victory. Hmm? What would that be like for me? I wondered.

The church was more of a chapel than a church, nestled in an older neighborhood, and built of stone with a quaint interior. The max capacity was a mere 200 parishioners. Centered behind the altar was an oversized mosaic of the Blessed Mother holding an infant Jesus. I assumed that was the Lady of Victory from whom the church derives its name.

I wasn't sure what drove me to attend church other than my son's wedding and guests traveling great distances, therefore all of us needed prayer. And this was a big deal, I gained two daughters-in-law in the same year.

Scriptures speak of a man leaving his father and mother to hold fast/cleave to his wife. Although this didn't happen between my husband and his parents, I was certain my apron strings weren't tight enough to do the same. The thought of it ruminated especially this week when my head and heart were full of emotions and trepidation because I still didn't have one word of my speech written.

Church began with an unassuming priest, Father Italiano, who immediately mentioned the mass intention. For those who don't know, Catholics pay the church for their loved ones to be recognized, mentioned by name and prayed for at certain masses. The priest then spoke of the saint for the day, it was St. Theresa of Calcutta. He encouraged us to call to mind how she lived the gospel of serving God with her hands and heart.

Mass went according to plan, all the while I focused on the mosaic with Mary and Jesus. Asking myself, what does it mean to be a woman of victory. I thought about the love Mary had for her son, the sacrificial love of sharing him with the world and releasing him to the cross for his divine plan. I considered the love I have for my children, and how I need to share them with others and the world, and that can be extremely challenging. I feared losing my sons to their wives. I didn't raise momma's boys, but we were close and sharing space in their heart with another woman was hard to imagine.

I related to Mary caving to God's plan of letting her son go and thought it best to surrender my sons the same way. The priest shared in his homily about St. Theresa reminding us to do small things with great love. Oh, that was good advice for the newlyweds. I was daydreaming about how caring St. Theresa was to the lepers who no one else would touch. My son's bride is a nurse practitioner with an incredible career in nursing who is not afraid to touch any ill human either. She is financially responsible, can fix anything, is adventurous, and my son loves her with all his heart. Aha! She is a woman of victory.

Suddenly, in that fairy-sized church the speech came to me. I felt the love of Mary and St. Theresa and Jesus and my son and my future daughter-in-law and the genuinely wise priest all swirling together in my mind. The cherry on the sundae came at the end when Father Italiano said, "Mass never ends, we are always to live the love and life of Jesus our Savior." Brilliant.

He was someone extraordinary. If every priest conducted mass like he did, every church would be filled to the gills. His authenticity and kind demeanor emulated every attribute of Jesus. His words were gentle, wise, and personal. His aura was that of a humble prophet who radiated love for us in the pews, and for God and all the saints. He connected with all of us from the beginning of mass until the very end.

My cup of gratitude overflowed for this unexpected divine gift so much so that I felt called to go to Confession offered at the end of this mass. I looked to this one-on-one with Father Italiano as an opportunity to seek his heavenly direction as I was about to become a mother-in-law for the second time.

This role was important, new, and somewhat challenging for me. Not because of the daughters-in-law I was gaining, but for the outspoken, over-involved mother and unfiltered woman that I am. I had been reading multiple articles about my role in the wedding and my position post wedding. Every article I read supported the old saying, "A daughter is your daughter for the rest of your life, a son is a son until he takes a wife." The advice was clear and repeated over and over, if you want to keep a relationship with your son, keep your mouth shut. UGH!

I shared with him about my sons' weddings and my desire to be a great mother-in-law. Without hesitation and before I said another word, he said "You will need to learn to bite your tongue."

I wanted to explain we are living in a new era of women having voices. He was an older man, so I assumed he still followed some old-fashioned roles of the sexes. He smiled and offered more wisdom about how important it will be to keep my sons in my life versus speaking my mind where it doesn't belong.

I respected his opinion and felt God had provided this whole experience for a reason. Who was I to not, at the minimum, monitor my strong viewpoints. My sons weren't children anymore and once they are married are to "…leave his father and mother and hold fast/cleave to/cling to/be glued to his wife…" (Mark 10:7 ESV) double UGH! Advice rooted in the holy word.

I recalled other scriptures highlighted in multiple colors and circled in my bible focusing on minding my mouth, "Set a guard, O Lord, over my mouth; keep watch over the door of my lips." Psalm 141:3 ESV. And, "He who guards his mouth and his tongue, guards his soul from troubles." Prov. 21:23 ESV. I envisioned a black leather muzzle guarding my mouth, and how that protective device should stop my words and preserve relationships. Message received.

I had a few days before the cleaving of my son to his bride, so I sprinted to my car to capture my thoughts and feelings and wrote the most perfect speech welcoming daughter-in-law number two to our family. Reserving tongue control for after the ceremony.

This was a providential postcard from the patron saint of mother-in-laws, St. Elizabeth. Thanks Liz. I didn't plan to go to mass, certainly not this church on this day. Yet it happened. I can't explain it. I can only be humbled and grateful for the holy cosmos loving me enough to bring it all together.

40

*"For I know the plans I have for
you, declares the Lord..."*

Jeremiah 29:11 ESV

The serendipitous and mystical experiences happened with unbelievable frequency and are impossible to plan for or orchestrate. One can never anticipate an experience that happens in one moment will parlay into something incredible in the future. These tapestries are woven by a power beyond our universe and comprehension.

While riding my bicycle over the summer, I saw an ad for a classic car show at our local church. The recent ones I had attended had been very disappointing with only a few cars and mostly current day muscle or luxury cars, not the true artwork of the classics. My expectations were low, but still wanted to check it out. I feel my dad's presence most when I am around classic cars and anything on wheels, and I jump at any opportunity to connect with him.

Usually, I peruse the show for vehicles from the year I was born or ones I remember my dad working on in our garage. As I approached the back parking lot where the show was happening, I was impressed with about 50 cars from various years, makes, and models. Be still my heart when I saw a Crown Victoria: it's the car my parents had when they were first married and the one on their shared gravestone.

While cruising the parking lot, I hear my father's voice saying the make and model of each car, "'57 Chevy." His spirit is so strong sometimes. Music from days gone by played overhead and a song that came on was the one about "If you're going to San Francisco, be sure to wear some flowers in your hair..." the special place where my daughter and I traveled, and of course where Bullitt was filmed. I miss my dad and want him with me to share in these moments.

With the confluence of my father on my mind and the accompanying music, I saw a Ford Thunderbird, one of his favorites, in purple, one my favorite colors with the license plate, "Ed's," my father's name. And of all the cars in this classic car exhibit, it was the only one with a matching kiddie car hitched to the back. Exactly the kind my father collected. He loved those little metal kid cars, and he loved his children and grandchildren and great grandchildren.

My dad and I didn't get to talk about anything spiritual while he was here on earth. But man, oh man, we are now. I have connected more with my dad since his passing than we ever did while I was growing up. I hope this recounting of my treasure hunt for spiritual truth and where to find God honors both my heavenly and earthly father. It matters to me that my descendants know how I developed a wildly wonderful relationship with the Holy Spirit. My faith hasn't come from a religion, it has developed from an unbreakable friendship with the Creator.

My Irish Heritage and ancestors comfort me with their Celtic spiral of life that believes spirituality is in the living of life, traveling the journey and finding joy in the ordinary, the heartaches, hopes, and dreams. I trust that God, and our loved ones encircle us with their presence, cradling us between heaven and earth.

I contemplated long and hard about the way I misconceived God as being distant and angry, most likely because my father and I struggled to connect. Looking back, I am sure I was the frustrating one to live with and get close to. He was my father, always concerned with and wanting the best for me, how sad it didn't click for me until after his passing. If only I would have known what was in his heart, his history, his thoughts.

What was my father's spiritual journey? What made me challenge the Catholic way from an early age and continue to question the doctrine, leadership, and dogma? I struggle to identify as a Catholic after learning of the rampant abuse and inconceivable cover up. This sickens me. Adding insult to injury is that women are forbidden to be priests and aren't recognized for their full discipleship. The church's history of corruption, abuse of power, and scandals are something I cannot ignore. If the Catholic Church were a business, it's actions would be an outrage to the community, calling for a boycott and criminal prosecution.

I understand why people have left the church; my hope is that they don't leave God.

I've experienced more disappointing church services than not, including a priest who forgot the paper notes for his homily and could not deliver one word without them them. He chuckled from embarrassment at first, as did the congregation, explaining he had those notes for 10 years. But when he could not offer any words of wisdom or scripture, the atmosphere turned awkward. I was appalled that this man of the cloth could not recall to mind or share one word of divine inspiration without his 10-year-old pre-written speech.

Another one that sends people running from the pews is when priests use Christmas and Easter as an opportunity to chastise the crowds for attending only twice a year. Berating parishioners when they are present doesn't make them want to attend more often.

I recall one mass which was both extremely unnerving and enlightening at the same time. My daily devotional that morning told me not to attend church. I should have listened when it said if you want to rest your soul, "don't go to church.... Because only God can give us rest, Jesus promises, come to me, all who labor and are heavily laden, and I will give you rest."

Ignoring that clear direction, I went anyway to one in an old familiar neighborhood near my first job out of college. The fond memories gave me a good vibe to attend this unfamiliar church over my lunch hour.

To respect the quietness of those already in attendance, I tiptoed my way down the aisle to keep the heels of my boots from echoing through the hallowed space and disturbing the peace.

It was listed on the website as "Low Mass in the Extraordinary Form." Not knowing what that meant, I assumed it was a low key, less ceremonial mass. Nothing could have been farther from the truth.

The priest walked out in full Chasuble regalia, including a green oversized sandwich board overlay with a colorful cross in full screen size, and a biretta (special hat). The 20 something altar boy received the hat from the priest and kissed it, then placed it on the table off to the side. The priest turned his back to us and faced the altar speaking Latin in a low murmur or silently in his head for the rest of mass. He only turned to the side a few times, and only faced us when it was time for Communion. I didn't understand or follow a word he said, I felt like an extra in a foreign film. I hoped it was good enough just to have my butt in the pew.

Upon communion time, we approached the altar where there was a short marble fence bordering the sanctuary from the rest of the church and cushions for us to kneel while receiving the Eucharist. I am finding other churches offering Communion the same way recently where parishioners receive the host directly from the priest. In this scenario, most people I noticed extend their tongue for direct deposit. Not me, I always offer my open cupped hands and it is given to me in my palm. Until this moment.

The priest brought the Eucharist toward my face, I lifted my hands to receive it and the priest shook his head no, prompting the altar boy to place the brass spatula under my chin. I raised my hands up and around the spill plate, bringing forth a seething look from the priest, and a more adamant head shaking no, nor would he release the Communion to my open hand. The altar boy, just as perturbed, leaned forward and shook his head no. Both men stood above and before me, refusing to give me the Body of Christ. I shook my head no and kept my hands in place. They refused to place the wafer in my now sweaty palm. I was astonished at the show of stubbornness at the altar.

I got up and walked out, without tiptoeing and without Communion. I clicked my heels hard on the wooden floor enjoying the loud echo among the stained-glass depictions of the life of Jesus. At the back of the church, I wanted to make a bigger noise, but I couldn't find anything to drop or throw. I shoved the door open with all my might to express my frustration.

I sat in my car, on this beautiful sunny day, contemplating how I missed my lunch for this and how wrong of them to refuse me the bread of life. A flood of anti-Catholicism feelings rushed through me. That priest acted like the very Scribes and Pharisees and Religious who made Jesus angry. Jesus never turned his back on anybody. He would never refuse himself to anyone who humbly came to him.

I was not welcome at this church and felt detached from the whole service. I wasn't an active participant, just an observer of a man-centered religious ritual. I felt pity for the people in attendance who believe this is acceptable. Although, I shouldn't judge someone else's experience with the divine. If this church brings others to God, who am I to say otherwise? Everyone's rhythm with the Lord is different. Ah, but if only everyone could experience Father Italiano who is welcoming, genuine, enthusiastic, kind, personable, then they would experience the true character and love of Jesus.

This experience weighed heavily on my heart for the people who do not know the truth, and I was grateful that I did.

With deeper contemplation on this experience, I could not believe I defied a priest just as he was giving me *the* Holy Communion. I refused the Eucharist. Did I turn away from God? Am I a horrible person?

It happened so quickly and unexpectedly, certainly not premeditated. The longer I thought about it, I didn't refuse God. It was as if the priest came in, performed a secret ceremony, and the people in the pews were irrelevant. When people are speaking to themselves or someone else in a hushed voice or secret language with his/her/their back to me, then I am not welcome or included in the conversation. This mass had the same act of exclusion.

It was disconcerting -- the Latin language, the haughty priest's back to us, the altar boy kissing his hat, and the priest insisting on putting his fingers in my mouth after he had just put them in a dozen other people's mouths. It was a germ thing, not an act of heresy.

I reacted as usual when I am angry, by walking away. It was a bold and brave act of defiance. Who knew I was capable of such a thing? I've come a long way on my spiritual walk to do this. Thank God that I know Jesus tore the veil when he was crucified. That wall between the altar and the people was removed, more than 2000 years ago.

I was both proud and perplexed that I walked away from that negative exchange. I am not a horrible person, but I am a lousy Latin low mass in the extraordinary form Catholic.

Not able to shake off the experience, I wondered if I should consult with an expert, or go to confession? Nah, this is between God and me. And worth a phone call to Lydia, who reassured me that it was man-centered, culture-centered, and it reminded her of the way the Sadducees and Pharisees acted toward Jesus. EXACTLY! She encouraged me to look for peace in a conversation with God from his word.

Our local pastor wrote in his newsletter once how a woman told him she missed the Eucharist while being away from mass during COVID. She said she didn't like being without God for that length of time. I take issue with her thinking she was without God because she wasn't at mass getting communion. God isn't exclusive to a wafer.

God is in the person who lovingly cares for the elderly or ill loved one, or the volunteer at the soup kitchen, or the neighbor who drops everything to help another through a crisis, or the friend who sits with you in the dark moments, or when holding the miracle of an infant in ones' arms, or rescuing someone stranded on the roadside, or from an abusive situation, or from harming oneself. God is in every living creature through shared love, compassion, and grace.

I must remember, there are good and bad teachers and school systems, yet we must attend school. There are good and bad managers and places of employment, yet we need to work. There are good and bad health care providers and hospitals, but we still need medical care. We shouldn't judge all restaurants by one bad dining experience. Likewise, there are are good and bad priests/pastors/preachers and churches. Still to worship with a body of believers is good for the soul, and I believe, if we want to change the system, we must stay in the game.

After all my seeking, I did not find God in a specific denomination's building. After all my searching for the right church, I discovered the church doesn't have walls at all. After all the doing, my works did not make me good enough. Because it was not about me; it was and is about living each moment aligned with the Divine expansive holy cosmos.

Investing my mind and soul in "praying without ceasing" through constant conversation and acknowledgment of God lay the foundation for holy experiences. Praising the divine in the moment and being grateful for the micro to the macro blessings ensures a spiritual rhythm, a divine dance. Spirit was always within; it was I who took decades to peel off the layers of religious nonsense to live a life aligned to the Creator.

I liken my mystical serendipitous experiences to a loaf of homemade bread baked fresh in the oven. The bread doesn't make itself. It requires a recipe, a trip to the grocery store, mixing ingredients, kneading the dough, time to rest and rise, shaping, proofing, and then baking. Divine moments happen most often when I've spent time meditating and praying with an open heart and curious mind acknowledging God in everything and everyone. Yet, there is not a single formula that everyone can follow to have the same outcome. We must find and follow our own spiritual relationship, like being in a waltz with the Creator, following a supernatural rhythm.

41

*"The Lord bless you and keep you, make His
face shine upon you, and be gracious to you...
and give you peace."*

Numbers 6:24-26 ESV

Since church attendance is only a fraction of my spiritual practice, I was puzzled by a recent inspiration to attend mass for seven consecutive days. Motivated by the scripture, "For seven days celebrate the feast to the Lord your God at the place the Lord will choose. For the Lord your God will bless you in all your harvest and in all the work of your hands, and your joy will be complete." (Deut. 16:15 NIV) The promise of blessings and complete joy nudged my soul to comply with the simple task of going to church for one solid week.

However, I doubted my divinely inspired plan two minutes into the first mass where the priest mumbled his words fast and low, making them inaudible. Which explained the severe quietness of the church where we could hear a pin drop. He mostly kept his back to the congregation. OY, another version of a low mass. This seven day observation was not off to a good start. During the whispered and hard to follow homily, doubt led my thoughts to ponder the real purpose of this trial.

During another mass, I felt the priest was in need of a career change since his ennui emanated more than his holiness. When someone stood at the podium, his head tilted off in the opposite direction while they read scripture or sang a musical interlude, his eyes rolled, and his legs fidgeted and shook like a school child eager for recess.

He didn't deliver a homily, the deacon did it for him, and the limp flick of his wrist while distributing communion without making eye contact emphasized his attitude of wanting to be anywhere but there. The only time he expressed enthusiasm was at the very end when he announced mass was over.

Luckily, there were priests the other five days who made the mass come alive and connect with the parishioners on a human and holy level. For instance, on Day Two, the priest asked us at the very beginning of mass, "What are you looking for here today at mass?" He grabbed my attention immediately as I had been asking myself that same question within minutes of following that little voice within. I was pleasantly pleased with the noon mass as he conducted the service with sincerity and his homily encouraged spiritual as well as self-reflection.

The Sunday of this seven-day escapade happened to be Epiphany Sunday, the day when the church calendar officially ends Christmas season and celebrates the three wise men arriving with gifts and the acknowledgment of God's manifestation as baby Jesus. I selected this specific church because of the mass time, location, and it advertised on its website contemporary music and American Sign Language. That was intriguing, I've never attended a mass with sign language accompanying the service. And by now, dear reader, it's obvious my love of and connection to good music.

Getting out of my car that morning in the parking lot of a church built in 1871, the church bells rang loud enough to vibrate the zipper on my purse. Upon entering the church, I was greeted by two people welcoming me with smiles and a "good morning!" and everyone was conversing throughout the pews with regular voices. No whispers. No quietness at all. It felt like I entered the social hall. The mood was light and engaging, and this made me happy. Mass proceeded with the usual pattern of readings, public confession, Glory to God, and Gospel. The ultimate attention grabber was when the priest mentioned his inspiration for the homily came from watching a movie on TCM! My heart pinged and eyes watered. This priest gets it.

The movie was "3 Godfathers" with John Wayne from 1948 where three outlaws became responsible for a baby when the mother died after giving birth. They promised her they would carry the baby to safety in the village of New Jerusalem. He likened the movie to the three wise men on the day of epiphany and the pure joy and transformation a baby brings into the world. In the movie, the baby saved the souls of the bank robbers, just like baby Jesus who saves and transforms our lives. Homily: two thumbs up.

One key prayer intention aligned with the main reason for writing this book. We offered prayers for the young people who are turning away from the church because it no longer serves a purpose in their lives. Yes, yes, let's pray deeply for those turned off by or have fallen away or deliberately left the church.

My newest philosophy on the role of the priests at mass is that they are like the teachers or professors of the class. The subject is the same, be it math, history, or anything, but who they are as a person and their passion and inspiration to deliver the service impacts the classroom experience. Everyone has had special teachers who make the topic pop with enthusiasm. I understand it is our responsibility to show up for class, be prepared, do our homework, and learn the information. But the instructor greatly influences the material comprehension and lessons learned.

The scripture that motivated me to attend church for seven days in a row, also said "the Lord will determine the location." Every location was an experience in and of itself, from historical buildings filled with opulence to modern day minimalism. The locations happened to be wherever I was traveling for work on that day.

I frequently use the website, "Mass times" where one can enter a location and it populates a list of churches and mass times within a certain mile radius. I rely on this while traveling and with my ever-changing weekend schedule. The randomness of the seven churches solidifies the spiritual universe holding me in its loving arms.

A few days prior to this seven-day excursion, I heard an interview on the radio with a scientist who studied the science of quitting. She mentioned several companies who did not make the necessary changes within their organization to maintain success. Most noteworthy: Kodak refusing to change its camera and film business model when digital came along, IBM not adapting its copiers, and Sears selling off two of its more profitable entities to remain in the flailing retail industry. The

Catholic church finds itself in the exact predicament as these businesses and it needs to change the model if it wants to put a tourniquet on the bleeding of parishioners leaving the church.

Combining parishes, retro altar boy attire, women covering their heads with lace, and bringing back communion distribution across the altar by the priests will not fix the serious issues. The leadership needs a close examination of real solutions to new ways of business, or the institution of the Catholic church will fall into the same lake that drowned Kodak, IBM, and Sears. Going backward never leads to moving forward.

The church needs shaken up, taken down, and demolished in order to rebuild and renew with spirit, not religion. It is much like the situation with our home repairs after the fire. One contractor painted over burnt wood and pieced the electrical and plumbing system back together when everything needed fully replaced. We can't paint over damage in order to be made whole, and we can't cover up the pain of abuse if there is to be healing. Moving priests around the diocese or country is as deceitful and wrong as the contractors who moved around our wiring and water pipes in the guise of fixing our home.

A few solutions: respect and honor women as Jesus did and allow us to hold leadership roles, end false teachings, acknowledge the wrongs of the abuses, criminalize their behavior, and prosecute those who abuse and those who allow it. And more than anything else, the church needs to focus on the grace, mercy, life, and love of Jesus. He fought corruption and religious nonsense, which existed since the formation of the church. He didn't accept it nor stand for it. Neither will I.

Faith is from the heart and not from sitting in a pew. The mass doesn't make me, I make the mass. God cares about us as individual divine creations and not about our religious rituals or labels. Consider how religion has ruined many lives with racism, violence, exclusion, and abuse of power. Contemplate the people who use the bible to mislead, judge, and beat others over the head. Which is worse? Not reading it or those who do and, with their own agenda, create hell on earth for millions.

Soon after the seven days of church, I listened to two audio books, one on my way out of town for a business trip and the other on my way back. Neither subject related to each other nor discussed business. The last day of travel began later than planned and my schedule was in flux as I arranged sales calls around potential noon mass. I was able to work church in my tight schedule and was pleasantly surprised when the priest began his homily with a story about how faith matters.

This caught my attention because one of the books I had just finished was about taking control of our time by prioritizing our life and scheduling around what "matters" most to us. I had been contemplating and listing what matters in my life over the last few days. It was confirmation of being on the right track.

Then he said, words can't always be exactly interpreted from one language to another, especially ancient Hebrew, Latin, and Greek. Those words brought me to full attention because that very morning the book I was listening to said, "sometimes there aren't adequate words to describe something and interpretations from different languages can vary greatly."

I appreciated the Almighty's perfect timing of my recent book choices with the time to read them and this exact homily. As I drove I65 South along the river from Toledo to Perrysburg, Ohio, I was seeking a fun Friday afternoon song to awaken the party girl in me. Then one very clear channel came through my dashboard with a non-denominational preacher talking about what really "matters" in this life. Pay attention to this, said the voice in my head.

The sermon was about how love is the only thing that matters in this life. He explained an ice sculpture is made from hard work, talent, a chain saw, and a creative mind. He likened how our lives are full of education, sports, work, playing an instrument, singing, hobbies, etc. And those things are good and necessary, and they make us unique, but they don't last. Only love lasts, the love we hold within us and the love we give away. What happens to the ice sculpture? It melts and is gone from this earth. As it is with us. When our lives are over, all of who we were and what we did will be gone.

The word "matters" and the question about what matters repeated itself again making my list of priorities clearer. Moments later after arriving in the quaint historic town of Perrysburg to get my second latte of the day, my feet froze mid stride. There was an *ice sculpture* exhibit throughout the town. Each business had its own display in front of its store. I thanked the Divine immediately for letting me know I was exactly where I was meant to be at that exact moment. God's message made as clear and solid as ice.

I started to share my experience on social media the following morning. When God nods this obvious it must be shared. But I was interrupted and became caught up doing my weekend chores and didnt get the opportunity to write about it. I posted my story of serendipitous series of events the following day. Minutes later, a friend who read it, text me that she had a disturbing dream the previous night and was upset all night trying to understand it.

After reading my post, she was encouraged to attend church. She found my message inspiring and was grateful for me sharing. I was equally grateful because she added another layer of mysticism with her note back to me about the dream she had the night before. One of the books which prompted my post was about dream interpretation, yet I never revealed the books I had recently read.

This post had to happen on that exact day, or it wouldn't have had the same impact on my friend. The timing of her disturbing dream and me reading those books and then posting about what matters all came together as only a loving holy cosmos can do.

There are thousands of books I could have been reading at that given time. Ponder the randomness of my choices: two audio books chosen because they were less than four hours in length, the radio program that I wasn't seeking to find, my work schedule of being in that town for that sermon, an uninterrupted car ride, the ice sculpture display, the day of posting on social media, and the morning after my friend's dream. It's nothing short of a marvelous miracle when multiple layers of divine timing align like the planets. Reminding me always, God is in full and total control of every moment, and I am always exactly where I am supposed to be, and the searching and surprises never end.

My epiphany has taken decades to sink in. It's not about a list of rules or the religious order in which one belongs or a perfect attendance record. None of that matters. It is about the way God's presence, grace, and wisdom have presented, unique as my DNA, exactly how, when and where it is supposed to happen. Divine mystery fills my soul with humility and gratitude as I am a home for the Holy Spirit.

Lucifer still lurks and is ready to prey on me, but as I pray without ceasing, Sheol has no hold on me. I declare to the devil, "Get your spurs out of this cowgirl!" After looking in all the wrong places for a sign and the perfect church, there was God in the bible, in my car, in the bizarre, in the music, the movies, the highs and lows, in every living entity. The Divine was, is and always will be found within our individual souls. I have gone from living in fear to living in faith, not a religious "faith," but true faith in the powerful living Creator of the universe.

It's not about being good enough for heaven. Thank God for Jesus, considering I fall short of perfection most days. It's who I found the Divine to be through the living word, nature, other people, in silent prayer with God, in solitude, and meditation. It was and is about the divine mystery of God's boundless treasure of compassion, constant presence, grace, and above all else...love.

42

"May you have the hindsight to know where you've been, the foresight to know where you're going, and the insight to know when you've gone too far."

Irish Proverb

"To err is human, to forgive is Divine," according to Alexander Pope. I mentioned before the importance of forgiveness, and although forgiveness is not listed as one of the spiritual fruits, it is a strong virtue, therefore when we extend forgiveness to others and ourselves, we are an extension of the Divine.

On my spiritual adventure to follow Jesus and lead with love, it includes forgiving others. When I forgive those who have wronged me or someone I love, there is peace in my heart and an unclogging of my arteries. It is a healthier way to exist in a world full of careless and cruel people. There have also been a few occasions when I needed forgiveness. Those situations are memorable, and usually not entirely my fault. Or at least that is my opinion.

One incident occurred after a long day of work when I had traveled in and out of town for three hours in the car including traffic and construction. While driving down my street toward our house I saw a giant turkey vulture devouring a cute bunny rabbit in the middle of the street just before our driveway.

I had never seen such a gory site, nor such a gigantic bird. Making the scene even more bizarre was that earlier that day I saw an albino squirrel in a tree above my car and a live possum under my car by my driver's side door. And this happened a stone's throw away from downtown. Of course, I needed a picture of this wild beast on my street. I took pictures of the other animals and capturing wildlife number three would complete my portfolio.

I pulled my car quickly halfway up the driveway. Far enough to be a safe distance from the ravenous turkey devouring his prey, yet close enough for me to get out and capture the nature scene with my camera before he flew away. I jumped out of my driver's seat, moving swiftly yet quietly toward the toddler size vulture pecking and poking at the flopping dead bunny carcass. I held my phone with both hands to get an amazing third photograph of the day.

When out of my periphery, I noticed the world starting to move around me. Was it my vertigo or was I dizzy from the excitement? I was not dizzy, and the ground was not moving. It was my car driving itself toward the garage where my husband's brand-new car, the one that took him multiple months to find, was parked and primed for a collision. I screamed and ran back to my car, jumped in and slammed my foot on the brake just as my car collided with the back bumper of his car.

Thank goodness I did not mistake the gas pedal for the brake pedal. I fully understand how this could happen in a moment of panic; my scooter incident was still fresh in my memory. I quickly threw my car into reverse and looked around to see who saw the incident. No one was outside or came to my rescue, hopefully nobody heard me scream or bumpers collide.

My heart raced and head pounded from my body's natural adrenaline coursing from scalp to toe. I could not believe I hit his car before he made the first payment. I asked myself, did I forget to put it in park or was there a recall on this vehicle for popping out of park? I cannot confirm or deny either.

Since no one was around, I discreetly checked out the damage. Thankfully, there was just a tiny little dent, and a mark the size of a razor blade. My next dilemma: do I tell my beloved spouse or let him find out another day, in another place and blame someone else for it?

It was best to let my nerves calm before making that decision or engaging in that conversation, if it needed to happen at all. After my blood pressure left the danger zone, I heard that little voice, the heavenly one, encouraging me to tell him the truth sooner rather than later. I agreed with that angelic direction. Yet, the very next second was direction from the logical left brain suggesting I wait for the right opportunity. I felt that advice made more sense. I planned to wait until later that evening when it was dark and difficult to see the minor damage. But, of course, my conscience would not stop pecking at me.

While my husband worked on his computer, I stood in the doorway between his office and the kitchen, and began my explanation with how stressed my life was, my overloaded brain, extra distractions pulling my thoughts in various directions and how the whole day was filled with extreme wildlife oddities right before my eyes. AND happening in the middle of our very own street. He was half listening, until I mentioned the part where I jumped out of my car which may or may not have been in Park. That made his ears prick.

As I explained the rest of the events, his thoughts brought forth redness in his face, a tightening of his jaw, and a more serious concerned expression. He looked away from his computer and up at me with one raised eyebrow and rested his poker face in his hand covering his mouth with an index finger. A familiar tactic to hold back words he may regret saying.

I made it clear the vulture did not attack me. His serious face was not relieved by this fact and that was a little concerning to me. I reassured him that his car was fine and asked him if he wanted to see my wildlife photographs. His response after a very deep and deliberate inhale, "Well I am glad you got the picture."

As we walked to the garage, I reiterated that I was unharmed in the situation yet could have been at any moment if the vulture turned to devour me. Still no response. Upon inspection, and with the benefit of early evening lighting, the scratch was minor enough to not cause a major marital incident. I apologized, he forgave me. Peace and harmony restored.

It is more than just the married moments. Every minute of every day, I am presented with an opportunity to live, act, react, and love like Jesus and come alongside people who are hurting or in need. I try my best to emulate Jesus' heart and actions toward others. Especially the way Jesus never judged anyone. He forgave, healed, prayed, performed miracles, walked away, and spent time in solitude and the wilderness. He spread peace, compassion, healing, wisdom, and love. Never speaking of peoples' sin, nor should I.

One day, one wonderful day, as I drove through the sprawling countryside of Ohio with my windows down, my curly hair crisscrossing my face, and fresh air filling my company car, I was gifted with another wave from heaven with the song "There Was Jesus." I smiled immediately because this song mixed my father's love of country music with my love of contemporary Christian music and it was a duet including one of my father and father-in-law's favorite singers, Dolly Parton.

I had heard this song before but this time, I listened more intently to the lyrics. With every stanza and certain words or phrases, my thoughts brought memories from our house fire and the restoration that followed and the testing of my faith. I also recalled the last days with my father, supporting my in-laws, and the heartache that ensued both our families.

I have known broken people and have been broken myself, and I realize nobody is perfect. I look back to when I felt God the most and it was almost always when my soul needed healing. I did not always see it in the moment, but now I can see the Divine hand on everything then and now, and it deepens my trust in a holy presence and proof of God's existence.

I was singing and shouting "YES" to every word of this song. Yes, to holiness everywhere, every day, in every way. Yes, in the odd and ordinary, in movies, on a scooter, in my car, when I am a sinner, and when I am a saint. Moments of giddy and goofy, and in the depths of agonizing pain. I am a child of God when I am wrong, worried, or in a wreck.

Exactly like Maren Morris when she sings "My Church" about finding redemption when she turns up the volume, my soul too is revived with every verse. The Holy Spirit runs through my veins, and I give her a big AMEN and exuberant ALLELUJAH!! Yes, this is my kind of church, in my car —singing, breeze blowing, sun shining, and free to follow the divine wherever! It is the one place where my soul is rejuvenated, my mind wide open, and my spirit holy hydrated.

There I was, traveling on the freeway in my company car, singing along with Dolly and getting in agreement with The Almighty Emmanuel. With each passing mile and repeated chorus, I shortened the journey from my head to my heart realizing, the Prince of Peace is within.

The journey with Jesus is much like riding in a car, with windows down, accompanying soundtrack, traversing on a never-ending joy ride through hills, valleys, sharp curves, sometimes hazardous weather and road conditions, other times it's all green lights. Just like Father Italiano says, "the mass never ends." Nor does the mystical experiences of knowing God.

I pictured a convoy including my dad on his Royal Enfield Bullet, my father-in-law in a 1959 Cadillac, and my grandparents in their signature gold Cadillac Coup de Ville. Alongside us, a posse on horseback with my Uncle Dale, and fellow Ohioans Paul Newman, Dean Martin, Clark Gable, and Doris Day. Most assuredly joining us on this joy ride was Steve McQueen in his 1968 Bullitt Mustang, and my dearly departed residents in the retirement village tour bus. And you, my faithful reader, riding shotgun with me.

Happy Trails

Epilogue

The spiritual journey never ends. Every minute of our existence we are presented with opportunities to be like Jesus through kindness, compassion, patience, forgiveness, generosity, and loving others as God loves us. It is never a one and done event. It is infinitely more than we can fathom with finite minds in our short time on this small earth. Change is here, together let's be a part of the new spiritual awakening of love, peace, light, and giving voice to the soul within. Thankfully, there are many wonderful people and resources willing to walk with us on our search for the sacred. I encourage those seeking enlightenment to spend time in silence and solitude, in prayer and meditation, in scripture - both written and nature, and welcome the mystery and expansiveness of a holy loving cosmos. Listen to and read books written by authors with open minds and hearts who honor the uniqueness of the Creator. Make connections with healthy and positive social groups, experiment with worship music, and, if possible, become involved with a faithful community who supports your individual journey.

Resources

The Wonder of God by Christine Sine

Sacred Earth, Sacred Soul by John Philip Newell

Soul Boom: why we need a spiritual revolution by Rainn Wilson

The Time is Now: a call to uncommon courage by Joan Chittister

Reforesting Faith by Matthew Sleeth, MD

This is God's Table: Finding church beyond the walls by Anna Woofenden

See the Good by Zach Windahl

Native by Kaitlin Curtice

Walking in Wonder by John O'Donohue

The Gift of the Unexpected by Jillian Benfield

The Soul's Slow Ripening by Christine Valters

Love Wins and *Everything is Spiritual* by Rob Bell

Being with God by A.J. Sherrill

A Holy Disorder of Dancing Monks – Facebook group

New Eden Ministry - newsletter by Justin Couts

Godspace – newsletter by Christine Sine

The Liminality Journal – newsletter by Kaitlin Curtice

anything written by Anne Lamott

L. A. McMurray's storytelling is a gift inherited through multiple generations of Celtic kin. Although her high school English teachers did not appreciate her ancestral creative voice and unique grammar skills, there was one English professor who told her, "You should be a writer." Those words had staying power whenever she took pen to paper, or fingers to keyboard. L.A. is an author, health promotions specialist, and spiritual traveler.

Her editorial on Doggy Yoga was published in The Bark magazine, and a personal essay about her 104-year-old friend was published in The Cincinnati Enquirer.

She has lived throughout Ohio, and currently lives in Cincinnati with her family and General Mills, a 100-pound Golden Pyrenees mix from Kentucky.

Cover images by Hailey Bollinger Photo
Author photograph by Hailey Bollinger Photo

 - @haileybollingerphoto